JOSSEY-BASS GUIDES
TO ONLINE TEACHING AND LEARNING

Learning Online with Games, Simulations, and Virtual Worlds

STRATEGIES FOR ONLINE INSTRUCTION

Clark Aldrich

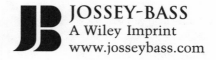

JOSSEY-BASS
A Wiley Imprint
www.josseybass.com

Published by Jossey-Bass
A Wiley Imprint
989 Market Street, San Francisco, CA 94103-1741—www.josseybass.com

Readers should be aware that Internet Web sites offered as citations and/or sources for further information
may have changed or disappeared between the time this was written and when it is read.

Jossey-Bass books and products are available through most bookstores. To contact Jossey-Bass directly
call our Customer Care Department within the U.S. at 800-956-7739, outside the U.S. at 317-572-3986,
or fax 317-572-4002.

Jossey-Bass also publishes its books in a variety of electronic formats. Some content that appears in print
may not be available in electronic books.

Library of Congress Cataloging-in-Publication Data

Aldrich, Clark, 1967-
   Learning online with games, simulations, and virtual worlds : strategies for online instruction /
Clark Aldrich.
      p.   cm.
   Includes bibliographical references and index.
   ISBN 978-0-470-43834-3 (pbk.)
      1. Education—Simulation methods.   2. Virtual reality in education.   3. Computer games.
4. Computer-assisted instruction.   I. Title.
   LB1029.S53A425 2009
   371.39'7—dc22

                                                                                        2009021642

Printed in the United States of America
FIRST EDITION

PB Printing   10 9 8 7 6 5 4 3 2 1

CONTENTS

To Muffy and Slate
With Special Thanks to

Mark Alexander
Storm Bear
Dennis Beck
Susan Blankenship
Jim Kiggens
Curt Madison
Rich Petko
Shannon Ritter
Sarah Robbins
Scott Traylor

PREFACE

A five-year-old girl visits a swimming pool at the beginning of the summer and is terrified. But with some playful challenges from her father, she works up her nerve to dip her toe in the water. She has entered a new world.

Slowly, she begins playing games on the pool stairs. She gets excited and engaged. She begins to splash with other children. She imagines the water is the ocean, and she lives in an undersea world, where her father is the king. In playing, she is learning how this new world works. The pool then becomes a comfortable environment for her and her friends to spend time.

Finally, she begins to deliberately challenge herself. It is not enough to be in the shallow end; she wants to learn to swim to the deep end. With the coaching of her father, she pushes toward the dark and cold, experimenting with strokes, overcoming the mouthfuls of water and finding the odd band-aid.

She gets frustrated and then excited with each new skill. It takes time, and progress is uneven. Two steps forward may be followed by one step back. But by the end of the summer, she has become a competent swimmer and could swim to safety in many different environments—other pools as well as lakes and beaches. She has learned skills that she will never forget.

This book contains the guidelines for instructors who will be selecting, planning, and implementing curricula using games, simulations, and virtual worlds in a distributed classroom environment (that is, where students are not face to face with each other or the instructor). This material focuses on both the front-loaded prep activities necessary for successful use and the instructor's role in a "learning to do" (as opposed to a "learning to know") course.

As with the pool example, it also takes into account the growing realization that these highly interactive virtual environments, while often successfully used separately, are increasingly and inexorably nested. If you squint hard enough, you can see that every game takes place in some type of virtual world, and every educational simulation is a type of rigorous game.

Further, instructors and students push the boundaries and functionality among all three. This means from a process perspective (as described in the subsequent chapters) there is overlap: the same techniques for increasing familiarity, giving instructions, or providing technical support with a virtual world are also relevant for games and simulations.

Here are the sections in more detail:

- *Part I* overviews some of the highest-level reasons for thinking about, caring about, and driving the use of virtual worlds, games, and simulations (to which we will collectively refer as *Highly Interactive Virtual Environments* or HIVEs). It describes the similarities and differences among these environments and explains the shift in mindset that highly interactive virtual environments require from both the students and the instructor.

- *Part II* details how to choose and use a HIVE, including how to identify an opportunity, select an environment or program, and use an environment effectively in your online instruction. It also offers strategies and techniques to assess learning outcomes.

- *Part III* covers larger issues of using a HIVE in your instruction, including advice on how to politically build a case for HIVE use to decision makers in one's organization.

- *The Epilogue* suggests that distributed education may drive the growth and use of HIVEs more than face-to-face classes in the near future.

My goal in writing this book is to be more practical than theoretical (although all the sections have theoretical edges to them). Using games, simulations, and virtual worlds can be a transforming experience for both the instructor and the student, so I want to be as specific as possible. But for those who are interested in the intellectual frameworks, there should be plenty of grist for those mills as well.

This text is also aimed at helping instructors meet the specific challenges and opportunities of highly interactive learning in distributed environments; it is not designed for face-to-face environments (also known as "real" or "meat" environments). However, I hope this book will provide some interesting insights and processes for them as well, especially about the different stages of deployment and the philosophies that are critical in each.

This book also talks quite a bit about developing a "culture of interactivity." We are living in an age when computer games are becoming more popular than movies, and social networking is becoming more compelling than magazines. Recalibrating the role of the instructor and balancing the student's need for certification, challenge, and accountability on one hand and for involvement and control on the other have become both more possible and more necessary.

Despite the image of complex educational simulations and vast virtual worlds, the content and philosophies in this book will not assume that students have a top-of-the-line computer and blazingly high-speed network access. Still, some will. So it will be my job to help you select the right solutions across technological, cultural, and content appropriateness from the different approaches presented here. Finally, I have used a very specific tone in this book that I have tried to match to the content area. As much as possible, it is written to be accessible and at times humorous. It is worth noting your own reactions to the approach, as it will line up with others' reactions to immersive learning and other game-like environments in general.

THE AUTHOR

As a designer, Clark Aldrich has created some of the most effective, celebrated, and innovative "soft skills" simulations of the past decade, including SimuLearn's Virtual Leader global product line (for which he was awarded a patent, is the most popular leadership simulation in the world, and was the winner of the "best online training product of the year"). SimuLearn's Virtual Leader (and the updated vLeader) is currently used in hundreds of corporations, universities, and military installations and has been translated into multiple foreign languages.

Most recently, he was the lead designer for a series of simulations for the Center for Army Leadership, which used a variety of short mini-game approaches to teach influencing skills.

Aldrich also advises many of the world's most influential organizations (private and government), and serves on over a dozen boards, including with the NSA, magazines, and universities, on educational and business analysis projects.

He is the author of four books, *Simulations and the Future of Learning* (Wiley, 2004), *Learning By Doing* (Wiley, 2005), *The Complete Guide to Simulations and Serious Games - How the Most Valuable Content Will Be Created In the Age Beyond Gutenberg to Google* (Wiley, 2009) and *Learning Online with Games, Simulations, and Virtual Worlds* (Wiley, 2009); and columnist and analyst. .

His work has been featured in hundreds of sources, including CBS, the *New York Times, Wall Street Journal,* CNN, NPR, CNET, Business 2.0, *BusinessWeek, U.S. News and World Reports,* and, among other distinctions, he has been called an "industry guru" by Fortune Magazine.

Aldrich was the founder and former director of research for Gartner's e-learning coverage. He graduated from Brown University with a degree in cognitive science, and earlier in his career worked on special projects for Xerox's executive team.

PART ONE

What Are Games, Simulations, and Virtual Worlds Really, and Why Should I Care?

Understanding Highly Interactive Virtual Environments

Imagine that you get a phone call at two in the morning, and you are told that you won a thousand dollars. But there is a catch. You have to spend it all before sunrise.

I don't have a profound analogy here, but wasn't it easy to imagine that situation? Humans effortlessly create virtual situations all the time. In our minds, we simulate shaking hands with the person we are scheduled to meet, and we plan different things we might say. Runners imagine the track and plan where to conserve energy and where to spend it. As we drive into a gas station, some of us visualize on what side our car's gas tank is. When we are given a new job, we plan for it by playing out scenarios, trying to understand our goals and foresee our potential actions and our barriers.

We also use virtual environments to do experiments. Einstein made progress towards his second theory of relativity by imagining he was riding a light beam. Programmers review steps of code in the shower, trying to figure out unintended consequences.

Schools, naturally, have long used highly interactive environments, if only a tad virtual. In classrooms, teachers use short games to introduce difficult topics, and mock trials have been the staple at law schools for decades. On sports fields, student athletes practice dozens of hours for every hour spent in a game.

Some of this practice is lighthearted and open-ended; other practice is intense and focused.

DO HIGHLY INTERACTIVE VIRTUAL ENVIRONMENTS WORK BETTER?

But do Highly Interactive Virtual Environments (HIVEs) work better for formal learning programs? Are they a fad, or are they the future? Are they the pet rock or the Internet?

The early evidence, both rigorous and anecdotal, seems to strongly suggest that highly interactive virtual learning is a permanent transformation of the educational landscape, coming out of its somewhat awkward adolescence and entering early maturity. This is due in part to interactive environments' ability to produce better traditional academic results.

Here is one well-documented typical example: Researcher Kurt Squire tested a simulation/game called *Supercharged*, developed at MIT by John Belcher and Andrew McKinney, to teach about electromagnetic forces. Using pre- and post-tests with control groups, he found that the participants in the control group receiving interactive lectures improved their understanding by 15 percent over their pre-test scores, while those who played with the game improved their understanding by 28 percent (Squire et al. 2004).

In another case, Dr. John Dunning, professor of organizational behavior at Troy University, discovered that students gave high marks to a popular required capstone public administration organizational behavior class using traditional linear media. However, when he surveyed multiple classes six months after the course was over, the knowledge and theories learned were not being applied in the workplace. To test the use of simulations, Dr. Dunning ran two organizational behavior classes. One class used the traditional curriculum based on case studies and term papers, and the other class used a leadership simulation. Six months after both classes were over, he again polled the students. The differences between the two classes were significant. Students who took the traditional class using case studies and reports, as was consistent with the earlier surveys, could recall some portion of class material. But the students who took the class that used the leadership simulation had significantly greater occurrences of being able to explain the material and, most importantly, being able to apply it (Aldrich 2009).

THE "WHY"

But it is still not clear *why* highly interactive virtual environments work. I suspect that we will be debating this for centuries. Here is a list of some current arguments, looking at the different components of interactivity.

Argument 1: Games as a Learning Tool

Games are a more natural way to learn than traditional classrooms. Not only have humans been learning by playing games since the beginning of our species, but intelligent animals have as well. Otters and African grays alike have been seen exhibiting what appears to be game-playing behavior. Lepper and Malone's "Making Learning Fun: A Taxonomy of Intrinsic Motivations for Learning" (1987) is a good high-level framework for fun elements. Games researchers Habgood, Ainsworth, and Benford (2005) explain that challenge, one of the motivations in Lepper and Malone's taxonomy, "depends on engaging a player's self-esteem using personally meaningful goals with uncertain outcomes. Uncertainty can be achieved through variable difficulty levels, multiple level goals, hidden information and randomness." Thus, the motivational effect of digital games comes from "the emotional appeal of fantasy and the sensory and cognitive components of curiosity."

Chris Crawford, in his book *The Art of Computer Game Design* (1984), suggests that games are "the most ancient and time-honored vehicle for education. They are the original educational technology, the natural one, having received the seal of approval of natural selection. We don't see mother lions lecturing cubs at the chalkboard; we don't see senior lions writing their memoirs for posterity. In light of this, the question, 'Can games have educational value?' becomes absurd. It is not games but schools that are the newfangled notion, the untested fad, the violator of tradition. Game-playing is a vital educational function for any creature capable of learning."

The optimal learning state is that of being in "flow." The term, coined by psychologist Mihaly Csikszentmihalyi (1990), refers to a mental state of immersion and clarity. Athletes call it "being in the zone," and the term has made its way into a number of fields including video game research. (For more information on flow's role in gaming, see Kiili 2005). Writers and computer game players alike talk about losing track of time for hours at a time.

Argument 2: Context and Emotional Involvement

Knowledge is useful only in context, and virtual environments provide a context, ideally similar to the context in which the content will eventually be used. (Gee 2003) This context can be specific or abstract, and it can also be emotional. For example, if the goal is to teach anti-bullying behavior when a person is highly stressed and feeling threatened, mirroring and simulating this emotional context is necessary for the new content to be absorbed.

Only if we have an emotional stake in the content does our brain release the chemicals in the amygdala and hippocampus necessary for memory (Ledoux 1998). This is why we remember a good novel better than a bad textbook. And in school, we best remember content when there is the fear of an impending test.

Combining the context and emotional arguments, many have argued that failure is necessary to learn (Klein et al. 2007; Keith and Frese 2008). Experimenting in environments where failure is acceptable is therefore necessary to learn and ultimately to develop cognitive resiliency.

Argument 3: Participation

Participation with content may be necessary for learning. In a famous experiment, Held and Hein (1963) exposed two kittens to nearly identical visual information. This was done by placing one of the kittens (the passive kitten) in a little gondola and linking it to a harness worn by the other (the active kitten) so that as the active kitten moved about and explored its environment, the passive kitten was moved in exactly the same manner. The result was that only the active kitten developed normal depth perception. The passive kitten, even though its visual sensory input had been nearly identical, did not.

The process of converting experiential expertise into linear material such as books and lectures strips out most of what is valuable in the content to begin with (Barrie 2001; Aldrich 2005). An analogy is that white flour, once bleached, loses much of the nutritional value of the original whole wheat. One can't learn to ride a bicycle, the saying goes, from a great lecture. And what is true for riding a bicycle might also be true of negotiating or stewardship.

CLARIFYING WHAT WE MEAN BY *HIGHLY INTERACTIVE VIRTUAL ENVIRONMENTS*

Of course, the more vague we are, the easier it is to generalize supporting evidence, but to less effect. Talking about *interactive virtual learning* broadly is like talking about television broadly. One could have said convincingly a few decades ago, "Television programs are a great way of entertaining a mass of people," but you or I, with hours of hard-earned experience under our belts, might now ask, "When you say television is entertaining, do you mean situation comedies, or dramas, or news, or commercials?"

Similarly, we need to get much more specific about different types of interactive experiences. As its title indicates, this book focuses on educational simulations, games, and virtual worlds. This, however, puts us in the epicenter of general confusion among students, professors, administrators, and, well, just about every one else. I have argued that they are connected, even nested. I would like to now argue that they are also very distinctive.

It is hard to have a conversation about either virtual worlds or educational simulations without someone inaccurately equating the two. And the person does this without even realizing it. For example, a classics department head may say, "Simulations are transferring the way people are learning. Just imagine *The Sims*, but around Greek politics. That is why we are looking into an island on *Second Life*." This is using a computer game as an example and putting forth an unstructured virtual world as a solution.

Figure 1.1 diagrams the relationship of virtual worlds, electronic games, and educational simulations. *Highly Interactive Virtual Environments (HIVEs)* is the encompassing term for the combined areas of educational simulations, games, and virtual worlds.

Virtual worlds are an infrastructure, analogous to a telephone or television system. Although some games are created and structured by instructors using an open-ended environment, the term *sims* in this chart applies to the portion of games (especially serious games) and educational simulations that are prepackaged media, closer in application to movies or magazines, and that try to influence students' behavior in the "real" world.

There are other vague terms floating about in Figure 1.1, including *educational simulations, virtual worlds, virtual classrooms, serious games, frame games, class games*, and *group challenge*. So here are some definitions and comparisons (we will define even more terms and get even more specific in Part Three).

Educational Simulation versus Virtual World

Educational simulations are structured environments, abstracted from some specific real-life activity, with stated levels and goals. They allow participants to practice

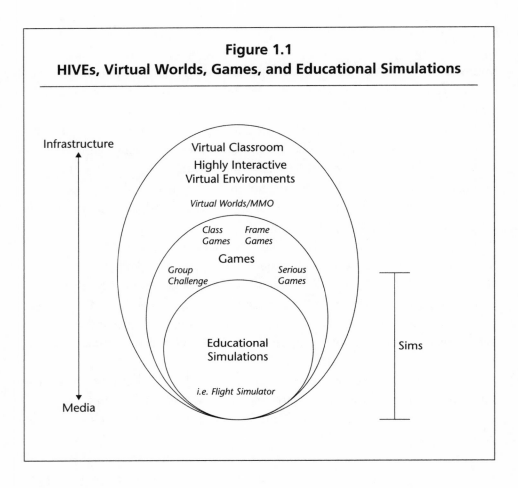

Figure 1.1
HIVEs, Virtual Worlds, Games, and Educational Simulations

real-world skills with appropriate feedback but without affecting real processes or people. For example, the Acton School of Business uses a rigorous educational simulation to teach students about designing effective production lines (Figure 1.2).

Virtual worlds are 3-D environments where participants from different locations can meet with each other at the same time. These environments can capture and convey enough social cues, such as body language, interactive props, and the look and feel of "real" surroundings to convince some part of the participants' brains that they are physically in this other world. Increasingly important, some virtual worlds also enable participants to build and otherwise change the environment. Linden Lab's *Second Life* is the best-known example of a virtual world, although many students have more experience with other examples, such as Active Worlds, Whyville, and ProtoSphere.

Figure 1.2
An Educational Simulation of a Production Line

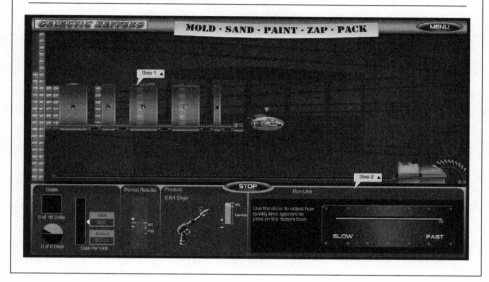

More like e-mail than Citizen Cain, virtual worlds are flexible but natively unstructured infrastructures in which many different activities are supported. These activities, as listed by Bloomsburg University's Karl Kapp, include the following:

- Entertainment
- Classes
- Meetings
- Virtual events
- Data visualization
- Prototyping/self-expression
- Replicating real-world facilities
- Virtual walkthroughs and tours
- Virtual mentoring
- Virtual recruiting
- Experiencing a disease state
- Creating machinima movies

People, once aware, seem comfortable with the differences between virtual world and educational simulation. The differences between the two types of sims—serious game and educational simulation—can be harder. These are obviously much closer than virtual worlds and educational simulations, but the differences between the two media are critical.

Serious Game versus Educational Simulation

Serious games are interactive experiences that are easy and fun to engage while building awareness, and *educational simulations* are more challenging experiences that rigorously develop skills and capabilities. Serious games usually require no coaching or outside help and even spread through word of mouth, promoted by people who enjoy playing them. (A *frame game*, a type of serious game, puts traditional academic content into an engaging interface such as a game show format.) An educational simulation, in contrast, often requires a coach or facilitator of some type and is part of a defined curriculum.

Perhaps the difference between educational simulations and serious games can be made clearer by their origin examples, the first examples that inspired the fields, as shown in Table 1.1.

The best example of an educational simulation, and also its earliest success and justification, is the flight simulator for training pilots. Flight simulators have many of the attributes desired in all educational simulations today. They are first person (what you see in the simulation is what you would see in real life); they directly relate to the needed skills; and their value is self-evident (in this case, to keep both pilot and plane from crashing).

Flight simulators impressively deal with both simple actions such as turning a flap or putting down landing gear and nuanced actions such as using the throttle. These actions are interfaced into complicated, dynamic, and intertwined systems such as wind shear and flying with a broken engine or landing gear. And these actions and systems are all coordinated toward the goal of landing a plane safely—and ideally at the right airport.

The hope and promise of the educational simulation movement are simple, if still somewhat speculative—namely, to use this interactive model increasingly for more academic and higher-level skills such as "understanding the decisions of a historical leader" or even "applying leadership."

In contrast, the prototypical serious game is Will Wright's brilliant *SimCity*. Players are highly entertained while designing and nurturing the cities they

Table 1.1
Comparisons of Educational Simulations, Games, and Virtual Worlds

	Educational simulations	Serious games	Frame games	Class games	Virtual worlds
Origin or Common example	Flight simulator	*SimCity*	*Jeopardy!*	*Rocks, Paper, Scissors; Scavenger Hunt*	*Second Life*
Primary learning goal	Deep skills	Awareness	Review	Ice breaker Microcosm/lab	Participation in and identifica-tion with real-time community, presenta-tion of 3-D interactive models
Primary success criterion	Accuracy	Engagement	Fun and relevance	Increased comfort level	Immersion
Technology requirements for students to access	Medium–High	Medium–High	Low	Low	High

evolved. It was intended to be (and published as) a game, and yet it has found its way into many academic curricula. It is easy to use (originally, it had a simple interface like a model train's), yet it presents complicated and interesting systems. Players have immense (albeit unrealistic) power, and they eventually become proud of their city in a way that few are proud of their homework assignments. They even view their cities as an extension of their own ethics and priorities.

Figure 1.3
An Influencing-Skills Sim

While playing *SimCity*, players also gain insight into urban planning. However, no mayor has ever prepared for his or her job by playing it. The content is abstracted to a point of high engagement, not transfer. The hope and promise of the serious-games approach is that many more examples will emerge that are just as addictive and perhaps a bit more educational.

So, in a nutshell, what is the difference between educational simulations and serious games? Serious games are how *you* want to learn, and educational simulations are how you want *your doctor* to learn.

Class Games

The next term it may be useful to define in this first chapter is *class game*, or *class activity*. This is a short activity to engage students (usually five to ten minutes, but sometimes as long as twenty minutes), typically "living off the land," or taking advantage of existing technology and infrastructure in the course environment. For example, an instructor might ask students to brainstorm what they want to get out of an upcoming class using only words that start with *P*. A class in *Second Life* might use a treasure hunt to help students learn about searching and teleporting. Or a virtual class using Adobe Acrobat Connect might ask students to text each other using the one-to-one messaging tool to learn three facts about their assigned buddy.

These class activities usually have one of the following goals:

- Ice-breaker, increasing comfort level between students
- Revealing current student knowledge (used either before a class to customize the content or after a class to diagnose the amount of content learned)
- Giving the students practice using the infrastructure
- Acting as a lab or microcosm for subsequent discussion and review

Ice-breaker, by the way, is considered an almost-derogatory term. Practitioners like to focus on how class games support *learning objectives*.

Other Terms

The last two terms are *virtual classrooms* and *group challenges*.

Virtual classroom tools provide an infrastructure for synchronous (same time, different location) classes and meetings, integrating voices, slides (including multi-student "mark-up" capabilities), text chat/instant messaging, application sharing, and various community control tools. They are commonly used today when students in a class are geographically dispersed. Virtual classrooms are highly interactive and are currently used as a platform not only for traditional lectures but also for many types of games and simulations.

Group challenges are activities where people have to work together to accomplish some finite activity. Typically, the activity requires participants to take on different roles and discover, rather than just apply, a solution.

The Importance of Using the Right Idea

We may have spent more time defining terms than some readers might prefer. But getting comfortable with the distinctions, and yes, even practicing using all of the defined concepts, will help you choose the best HIVE for your learning goals and will also facilitate conversations with all stakeholders.

Some people may ask, "Why isn't what we're doing in our online teaching and learning enough?" The next chapter will explore the importance of interactivity in the learning process and how HIVEs can be used to foster that sense of interactivity.

Embracing Interactivity

Last chapter, we talked about different definitions for infrastructure and media that make up highly interactive virtual environments. Before going too much further, it is worth zooming out to define—no, to embrace—the concept of interactivity itself. Many conversations around interactivity in formal learning programs rest on the tools. Does WebEx allow polling? Can you have threaded conversations in the virtual world of ProtonMedia's *Protosphere*? What if you gave keypads to members of an audience? Those are all good questions.

But there is a much higher and more fundamental challenge. To successfully deploy HIVEs (and perhaps even to be successful with any educational program), we need to nurture *cultures* (and then skills sets) around *interactivity* that are independent of any technology. For example, in a true culture of interactivity, it is painful if anyone, including the instructor, carries on a monologue for long. The goal is always a conversation not a presentation (Feel free to insert your own "sage on the stage/guide on the side" cliché here, but I promise we will get more specific in this and subsequent chapters.) How many presentations have you attended where someone proclaimed his or her desire for an interactive session, only to talk for the next 55 minutes?

In a true culture of interactivity, the learning goals are not just the traditional "learning to know" type, but also "learning to be" and "learning to do." Students meet their needs to understand themselves better (including their role in the community and how to take advantage of their unique strengths) and to be able to do new things (such as being a leader or using project management skills), not just hear facts.

Enabling this sort of interactivity is challenging for an instructor (or a corporate manager or senate investigating committee, or . . .). To be successful, instructors have to give up control. They have to be less efficient with time in the short term. They have to know more but say less, especially when students are flummoxed. They have to cover less ground but ultimately teach much more.

INTERACTIVITY LEVELS 0 THROUGH 6

For the vocabulary and expectations related to levels of interactivity, let's start with a linear rubric. It should be useful, in practice if not in theory, for all formal learning programs, including face-to-face and virtual. Like the Richter scale, it is logarithmic—each level is double the interactivity of the level before it.

Pre-Game Levels

Here are the early levels with minimum interactivity.

Level 0:   In Level Naught, the instructor speaks regardless of the audience. This is the proverbial talking head, often supplemented with PowerPoint slides. Most books and some lectures fall in this level. The goal is to cover as many points as possible in the given time. Level 0 material is easiest to prepare for a novice instructor, or anyone with bombastic tendencies.

Level 1:   In Level 1, the instructor pauses and asks single-answer questions of the students, such as "What is a dodecahedron?" When the question is correctly answered, the class continues. Many traditional e-learning courses fall here, as well as workbooks.

Level 2:   Here, the instructor tests the audience and, depending on the collective response, skips ahead or backtracks. A good preacher might poll his or her audience ("Amen?") and, based on the enthusiasm of the response ("Amen!") or lack thereof ("Amen . . . "), decide to accept agreement and move on or to linger and make a case. This might require preparing three hours of material for a forty-five minute sermon. (For a military presentation, replace "Amen" with "Hoo-ah.")

Level 3:   The instructor asks multiple-choice questions of the audience, and students may have the opportunity to defend different answers. Or the instructor asks real-time polling questions for data. Or an open-ended student chat room paralleling the presentation may periodically surface an issue that the instructor addresses. Asking students to use the "raise their hand" button to answer a polling question is a Level-3 activity. Questions such as "How many people agree with . . . ?" "How many students would do A instead of B or C?" "Give an example of an onomato-poeia" or even "How many students think the weather is nice today?" get students used to engaging. Ideally, a synchronous (same-time) formal learning program should involve polling or other micro-engagements at least every 10 minutes. Most branching stories (simulations with multiple-choice decision points) also fall here.

Game Levels

Now, things get interesting. At Levels 4–6, the culture of interactivity changes the traditional teaching process.

Level 4: Students engage a lab or other process activity that typically has a sin-gle solution, such as putting together an engine, making muffins, or gerryman-dering a district. Level 4 can also include minigames (15- to 60-minute online sims that require competency, successful understanding, use of a system, and encourage a limited amount of creativity). The role of the instructor is starting to be more coachlike.

Level 5: Students engage an open-ended lab or other activity and create unique content. Students can express individuality and cleverness that they may want to share and show off, often via screenshots in a chat room. However, *most* solutions will fall into fairly predictable patterns if the activity is done enough times (although there will always be some Mozarts that startle and impress). This level includes the analysis of case studies, the use of interactive spreadsheets (a type of mathematics-based simulation, such as running a liquor company, described later), practiceware sims (a flight-simulator), and the playing of most complex games, including real-time strategy (RTS) and tycoon games.

Level 6: Students engage in a long, open-ended activity, such as writing a story or creating and executing a plan. Where the class will end up is unpredictable, even after dozens or hundreds of iterations. At this level, the instructor is almost completely an enabler, a coach/facilitator, a resource, even a spectator. Students may use blogs and microcosms and engage multiday role-plays, including virtual-experience spaces to manage and host role-play artifacts.

Although the examples of the six levels use technology, this rubric can be applied in a traditional classroom. What's important is the culture of interactivity, not the technology. For example, many of the Thiagi Group's training games (http://www.thiagi.com/games.html) will engage an audience without using much, if any, technology or even any consumables.

The implication is not that Level 6 should always be used. Ideally, most programs will start at Level 1 and then transition to Levels 3, 4, 5, or even 6 as quickly as possible.

Level 7 and Beyond   Are there levels beyond 6? Sure. The manner of grading, the types of activities used, the chunking of the materials, and even the curricula itself can be directly impacted by the students.

Here is how Brock Dubbels[1] describes using a face-to-face simulation and developing a culture of interactivity in the classroom. He will begin talking about Level 6 and show how that can shift to Level 7

I teach fluid dynamics and aerodynamics to "at risk" high school kids. I try to appeal to the things that might be interesting.

I know if I talk about certain words too early like resistance, displacement, or friction, the students are going to check out. So what I say instead is "Next week I'm bringing in my wading pool. And we are setting up the first lake this school has ever had. And we are going to have a boat race. To win the boat race, you have to win in one of four categories: speed, weight-bearing, maneuverability, or general purpose."

The students get a general idea of what their goal is. But they also realize that they will need things that they don't currently have.

Then I ask the question, "If you were to learn about boat building, how would you like to do it?" I begin to elicit people's responses. This helps me get a sense of prior knowledge. By doing this I've accomplished building interactivity from the beginning, and I also start introducing the concept

[1]Dubbels is a middle-school teacher and instructional designer and also teaches a course called "Video Games as Tools for Educators" at the University of Minnesota. As a researcher, Brock is affiliated with the Center for Cognitive Sciences at the University of Minnesota, and specializes in reading comprehension, engagement, and exploring new technologies for assessment, delivering content, and investigating ways people approach learning.

of choice. Of course, from my perspective, all of the interactivity is prestruc-tured. But the students don't know they're being shepherded. They just know that they're going to a better pasture.

Then I ask the question, "What would you build if you knew you couldn't fail?" This gets their imagination involved. This engages their ability to visualize.

Then we start building communities. I ask people to share "perfect world stories." For example, I might say, "If you are to build boats, and you are to have a race, and I will provide all of the materials for you, what would that look like? How would you build your boat? Are there other races you'd like to have?" We start tapping into the excitement.

Most people like the default model that I have up on the board. But there are always some people that won't engage unless they have some sense of choice. They won't engage unless they are heard. I look at these people as desperately wanting leadership, and not willing to involve themselves unless they have a leadership role. So, I try to get them into a leadership role as fast as possible. This is consistent with the research around affinity groups for communities of practice. The question is, how do you distribute leadership and not hoard it?

What we might do is write up on giant sheets of paper the various ideas, and give people votes. We can have the class control the experiment.

The nice thing about this phase is, if it is done right, it eliminates one of the biggest criticisms of any kind of formal learning, which is that it's not relevant and not interesting. The students can control both.

In some cases, the students can even determine how I am going to grade them. Generally they don't deviate very far from the guidelines I put up for them. But we are creating education that is co-created, not top-down or hierarchical. So we might have a wiki that explains the day-by-day curricula, and I give students the ability to change that up to the morning of that day's class.

INTERACTIVITY LEVELS AND LEADERSHIP MODELS

Given this focus on interactivity, including the taxonomy of levels to measure our-selves (and much more amusingly, our colleagues), some might ask, why is interactivity with students so critical anyway? We may sense the value of interactivity intrinsically (it certainly matches our own best educational experiences), but how do we frame the extrinsic benefit? How can we justify our belief? Where's the beef?

The answer may best explained by leadership theory (Yukl 2002). As we increasingly understand, the level of interactivity used in a formal learning program directly affects the students' long-term relationship with the content. This is because the levels of interactivity correspond to specific leadership styles, which predict surprisingly well the subsequent effect on the so-called "target of influence" (in this case, the student).

At one extreme, interactivity levels 0 through 2 correspond to the three leadership styles of *pressure*, *legitimate authority*, and *directive*. The message communicated is "You will do this and do it now, because I can make you. If you don't, you will get in trouble, such as a failing grade or defenestration." At best, the leader—in this case the instructor—can gain short-term student compliance through these techniques. More likely, however, the student reaction is closer to *reactance*—instinctive emotional rejection of a situation where only one path is given and the target of influence has neither choice nor say.

By Level 6 (or 7 or 8) in our interactivity scale, the leadership style, formally defined, is *collaboration* and *participation*. It is more akin to the instructor saying, "I can't do this alone, and I need your help. In fact, I trust you to do it, and please let me know how I can help you." This is how one gains commitment and ownership in any leadership situation, especially teaching. The students both remember content longer and use it more.

Developing a culture of interactivity and using highly interactive virtual environments can be done separately. One is not necessary for the other. But the two together create the biggest intellectual payoff.

Sims: A New Model of Content

The culture of interactivity described in the last chapter is a necessary foundation for best using highly interactive virtual environments. But over time, taking advantage of the opportunity of interactive environments requires a new philosophy of *content* as well.

Simply said, and write this on a yellow stickie and put it next to your computer, *we don't want to just re-create the classroom in a virtual 3-D world.* Thankfully, we can still build upon our legacy of *learning to know* (we understand how to grade a term paper and present a lecture) to increasingly add a rigorous approach to *learning to do* (such as evaluating a performance in moot court, or in a team building project).

In Chapter 1 (Figure 1.1) we defined *sims* as that portion of games that includes all prepackaged educational simulations and many serious games and group challenges, presents some abstracted world and the player's role in it, and has some transferability to the productive world.

Sims, including stand-alone and as part of a virtual world, are a form of media that use *simulation elements* to model an abstracted reality, are surrounded by *pedagogical* and *game elements*, and are organized into *levels* to make the experience more instructional and enjoyable. Let's zoom in for a bit more detail. Here is how each of these pieces should be combined and calibrated.

SIMULATION ELEMENTS

Simulation elements are the most important part of a sim. They directly correspond to learning goals, and they model and present an abstracted reality. They include three layers:

1. Real-life *actions* (things that the student can do), reflected in the interface (see Figure 3.1) and accessed by the keyboard, mouse, or other input devices

2. How the actions affect relevant *systems*, including maps, buildings, communities, and even chemical processes

3. How those systems produce *feedback* and *results*

Figure 3.1
The throttle in the bottom left of this boat sim is an example of a calibratable action interface.

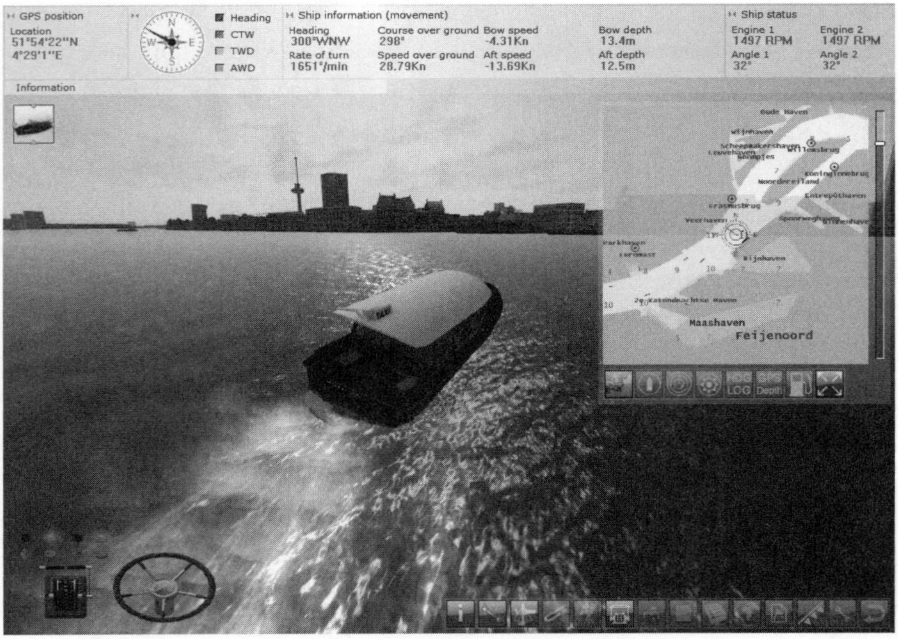

Here's an example of these three layers. For a politician to be elected (the *results*), he or she must do a lot of *actions*, such as make speeches and promises, schmooze with donors, be photographed sitting on straw and playing the banjo, and otherwise use media. But the politician must understand how his and others' actions impact the underlying (and often invisible) systems—such as party power structures, code words for hot topics, and electoral maps—to ultimately turn those actions into the desired result. Further, this system is changing with the emergence of social networking and even crowdsourcing, which has been used in politics most notably by MoveOn.org.

Simulation elements are almost always simplified in a sim and sometimes considerably so. Bloomsburg University's Karl Kapp, with his class building an emergency response sim in *Second Life*, used a photograph of a city street as a background to capture the feel of the environment.

However, a sim consisting of only simulation elements is incomplete. It is really boring and dry (think shredded wheat without milk) and takes a very long time to play out. Further, students don't always know what is going on. They may fail in the experience and not know why or, much worse, they may succeed and not know why (*failing up* may be a common path for many successful corporate types, but the same lucky sods resent un-understood success in a sim). In other words, simulation elements are like life. Therefore, in a good sim, they need to be mixed with

- game elements to make it engaging (the milk and sugar for our shredded wheat) and
- pedagogical elements (including coaching) to make it effective (such as the list of ingredients and nutritional value, perhaps with a comparison to *Cookie Crunch* Cereal).

GAME ELEMENTS

Game elements are techniques that motivate people to want to engage an experience, outside of any intrinsic motivation. A game element can be a beautiful campus in a virtual world or a giant explosion. It can be an award, a situation with no pressure, a chase, or a treasure hunt. Game elements also include compelling contexts, cool graphics, and futuristic designs as well as the ability to adjust the difficulty level, to try for ever-higher scores, and to choose an on-screen character's appearance.

Some game elements can be simple to spontaneously implement. Instructor-imposed constraints that force students to be clever and self-expressive are always a good idea. For example, students might be instructed, "Describe the most important thing learned in that last section, but do so in six syllables." Some instructors of virtual classrooms have played with instant prizes, such as Amazon gift cards. Others have used the "virtualness" of the situation for a little humor, such as giving out "virtual candy" to students as a recognition of success.

Game elements can do a lot of good in sims. Game elements drive engagement. They can build good will, which is often then transferred to the content itself. They can lower tension (so assessing with a game show might be more accurate than assessing with a test). In fact, the genre of frame game that we discussed in Chapter 1 is the result of almost pure examples of game elements.

But game elements are also controversial. Both parents and teens look at them suspiciously and often for very good (if opposing) reasons.

- Game elements dilute the learning. They take up developer time and they take up end-learner time, ultimately taking resources away from the primary content, including learning objectives.

- They are subjective. What is fun for one person, such as gambling or shopping, clowns or monkeys, can be tedious or scary for someone else. Different game elements appeal to people of different cultures, ages, and genders with different experiences and needs.

- Game elements can also reduce the fidelity of the learning. A developer can make things happen faster or more dramatically or abstract tedious steps, which increases the fun but at the expense of accuracy.

- Learners can often leverage "fun" elements to "game" (read that "cheat") the sim.

- Game elements like competition predictably and almost inevitably focus students on getting a high score rather than on learning the material.

- Badly implemented game elements can be awkward and, well, just lame. I have carefully included some ineffective attempts at humor throughout this book to help give you just that student experience.

In many ways, game elements are part of the aesthetic of a sim. It is important to think about the design of game elements—for example, the length of time a student might have in a fast-moving game or the sound that objects make when they hit a wall. They set the tone.

Too few game elements result in a boring, dry experience, and too many game elements create a silly and distracting activity. As a rule, the more one cares about content, the more one is intolerant of game elements. If you need to know how to evacuate a smoke-filled building, the last thing you want is to play a word jumble to get the information. Consequently, serious games tend to use more game elements than educational simulations do.

The purest example of a game element in an academic environment is the grade. Instructors use the promise of As or Bs and the threat of Cs, Ds, or Fs as carrots and sticks. While grades are not necessarily fun, instructors use them to ensure students pay attention. And like other game elements, grades can subvert learning by overshadowing (and even repelling) students' interest in the content.

PEDAGOGICAL ELEMENTS

Imagine a perfect friend next to you as you are learning to drive. She would start off by giving you a lot of information. But after a few hours, she might become increasingly quiet, just making some small, relevant observations. "Watch the car ahead of us. You are getting a bit close." Or "The next exit is ours." Or "That was a squirrel."

Pedagogical (also called *didactic*) *techniques and elements* surround an experience, ensuring that a participant's time is spent productively. Pedagogical elements in real life range from one-way street signs and labels on food packaging to the helpful neighbor who knows more about electricity than you do. They represent the codification of and access to context-specific knowledge.

In sims, including stand-alone and as part of a virtual world, pedagogical elements include training levels and islands, briefings, in-game tips/directions/signs, buddies, exposition, diagrams, workbooks, graphs, highlights, coach/facilitators, background reference material, the ability to go back and play again, and After Action Reviews (AARs).

In educational experiences, pedagogical elements help the learners

- know what to do;
- know how to use the interface;
- avoid developing superstitious behavior, such as believing they are influencing something by a particular action when they are really not;
- see relationships between actions or items faster;

Figure 3.2
A Virtual Coach Gives Players Advice

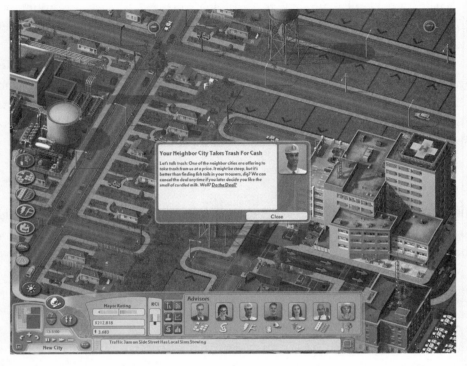

Source: Electronic Arts SimsCity Franchise

- work through frustration to get to resolution;
- try different approaches; and
- apply lessons to the real world.

Pedagogical elements have to calibrate the challenge by neither giving too much or too little help. If there is too much instruction, sims become fancy workbooks. But for a student, having too little pedagogy is like waking up in the middle of the night with no clock in the room.

Pedagogical elements take the place of the wise instructor (and can literally be a virtual mentor/supervisor/guide), watching, commenting, pointing out key relationships, and knowing when not to say anything. Typically, the larger the

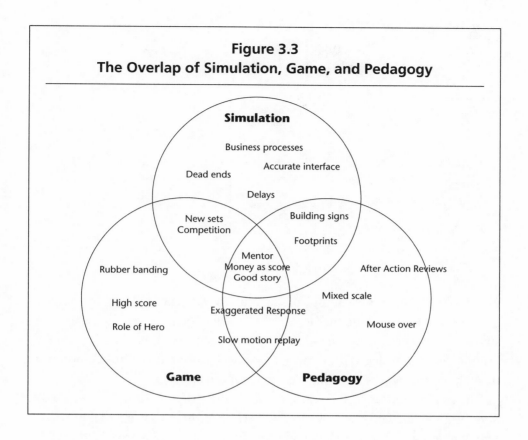

Figure 3.3
The Overlap of Simulation, Game, and Pedagogy

Simulation

Business processes

Accurate interface

Dead ends

Delays

New sets
Competition

Building signs

Footprints

Mentor
Money as score
Good story

Rubber banding

After Action Reviews

High score

Mixed scale

Exaggerated Response

Role of Hero

Mouse over

Slow motion replay

Game

Pedagogy

audience using a sim (as a ratio to the instructor), the greater the reliance should be on prepackaged pedagogical elements.

The three elements of simulation, game, and pedagogy are presented in this chapter as distinct. They have different roles and value to a successful sim. But just as a great film director can successfully combine exposition, character development, and action, so too can good sims combine simulation, game, and pedagogy (see the overlaps in Figure 3.3). For example, because money is (often) the sign of success in real life, money-as-score can let players know they were successful (even if just in the short term) and can be fun.

TASKS AND LEVELS

Finally, just as books are broken into chapters, pages, and paragraphs, so sims are best organized into tasks and levels to create incrementally more challenging

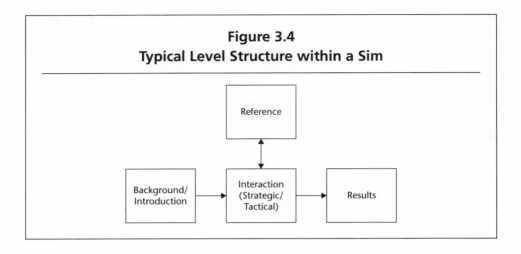

Figure 3.4
Typical Level Structure within a Sim

practice environments. Typically, progressing to the next level requires success-fully demonstrating some mastery in the last. For example, in a virtual world, students first entering the new environment spend time in an asynchronous training level. In order to pass through and teleport out, they must demonstrate their ability to navigate, manipulate, and communicate.

The framework for each level may include the structure shown in Figure 3.4. Sims begin with a fairly non-interactive briefing (either by an external instructor or by the sim itself), where story and task/objectives/missions are introduced.

The participant then progresses to the *interaction* phase of the level. There may be a strategic decision first, such as where on the map to go next, what items or units to bring, or what power-ups, if any, to use. Then comes the core game-play. Here, players perform actions and get feedback. Throughout, there may be constant access to reference material.

Finally, at the end of level, there may be a harder challenge. This is followed, where appropriate, by formal feedback such as an After Action Review (AAR).

These debriefings can be automated or done by a coach. Bloomsburg University's Karl Kapp debriefs with his twenty students after every exercise in *Second Life*: "I have everyone sit down at a large virtual conference table and ask questions. You use the same facilitation skills you would use in a face-to-face environment, but you have to be more acute because you are only picking up audio cues. People may be bored during a session, but you can't see them look at their watch when they are in-world. And you have to ask more basic questions and then layers of questions."

GENRES OF STAND-ALONE SIMS

The sim information construct that we just went through can seem overwhelming. Luckily, sims have settled into genres, which are predictable combinations of interfaces, systems, and goals. Once students have engaged one example of a genre, it is typically much easier for them to engage the next example.

The following list of genres is an analysis of patterns of today's stand-alone sims. But the way they present information and the best practices to use them are increasingly making their way to sims that use a virtual world as a platform.

Genre 1: The Virtual Lab

The first genre is virtual labs. In virtual labs, students are given challenges to solve with realistic online versions of objects or applications. For example, a chemist may walk in the room of a virtual lab and see a smoking beaker. He or she may have to perform actions, such as adding other chemicals or turning off the stove, to avoid disaster. Of course the lab could just as easily feature a pregnant walrus, a bubble machine, a mushroom farm, or a vat of pollywogs.

What is interesting about that virtual lab model is that the interface is unabashedly part of the content. What you do, where you do it, how hard you do it, and how long you press the "turn the wrench" button or to what you attach the whippletree matters a lot; it is not just a matter of clicking A, B or C. Kinesthetic learning is going on as well as content learning. The virtual lab focuses on the actions of the participant in a realistic setting that transfer nicely to real life.

Virtual labs were an early success and established momentum for stand-alone sims, and now they are doing the same for virtual world sims. Only in this next iteration, in today's virtual worlds, the students are just as likely as the instructors to build the labs.

Genre 2: Frame Games

With the goal of making learning fun, frame games engage students in familiar games and puzzles such as Wheel of Fortune, card games, and word games, but important pieces of knowledge or task-based content replace trivia or icons. For example, the player might play hangman but with medical terms. While making heavy use of game elements and being more diagnostic than instructional, frame games work well to support compliance programs and other situations where broad audiences need to cover basic information.

Plenty of sim purists eschew frame games as the red-headed stepchild of HIVEs. They run the risk, plenty say, of trivializing the subject matter. Yet I just included them in a recent sim I designed. Here's my thinking.

The program was about four hours long. Linear content—traditional presentations of key models and ideas—took up about thirty minutes. Most of the rest of the user time was spent in simulated scenes that fell more into the slightly dry category of educational simulation than serious game. They were hard and required serious focus.

So I decided, twice in the sim, to present a fast-moving, highly interactive review of some of the key concepts. In a variation of *Tetris*, quotes fall from the top of the screen, and players have to identify them correctly. If they do, they

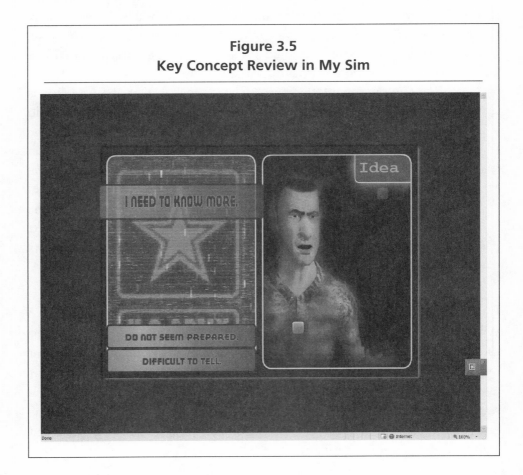

Figure 3.5
Key Concept Review in My Sim

disappear. If they do not, they build up and the student has less time to make the subsequent identification. If the player gets seven wrong, the game ends.

To me, this addition takes advantage of the positives of frame games (fast-moving and entertaining reviews of key concepts): they can both test absorption of content and break up the course nicely. Also because I used roughly the same game twice, after students learned the game, they could easily engage the content again. I would further argue that students will review and demonstrate knowledge of more content more quickly using a game like this than they would if they were faced with a multiple-choice review (and they'll have more positive attitudes toward the course as well).

Most importantly, the interactive reviews do not come at the cost of the more rigorous simulation experiences before and after. Rather, they set up future success in the sim, which should set up future success in the real world.

Genre 3: Branching Stories

The next genre is branching stories. Did you ever read a *Choose Your Own Adventure* book as a kid? These are the same thing. A *branching story* is an educational simulation genre through which students progress by making a series of multiple-choice decisions that affect the outcome.

Students start with a briefing (such as, "You are an ornithologist in North Dakota, and just found a moist...") . They advance to a first multiple-choice decision point, or branch (see Figure 3.6). Then, based on their decision or action, they see a scene that provides some feedback, advances the story, and then sets up another decision (such as, "As you come over the hill, you see in the field below you a series of crop circles. Do you (a) investigate, (b) go back and call for help, and (c) stay where you are and observe what happens?"). Students continue making decisions, traversing some of the available branches, until they either "win" or "lose" by reaching a successful or unsuccessful final state. Students then get some type of After Action Review.

Also typically but not always, actions are invoked by the player's character saying different statements to direct other people.

Branching stories can be presented in any combination of text, full motion video, pictures, and sound, and they can take on an almost cinematic quality. Branching stories can be designed to be used multiple times. When this is the case, the program might use breadcrumbs to show what decisions the player made last time.

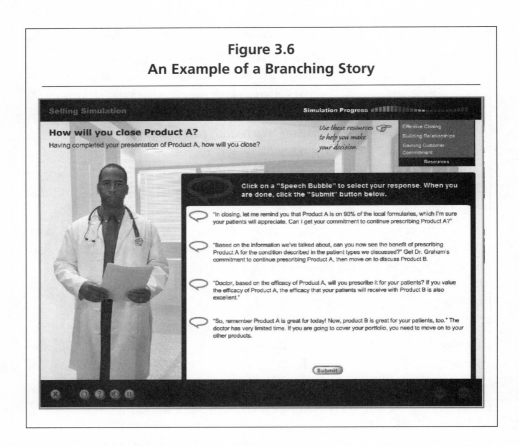

Figure 3.6
An Example of a Branching Story

The simplicity of the interface is both the greatest strength and greatest weakness of branching stories. They are easy to push out to students. They are as stand-alone as sims get. The choices are obvious. They most likely have built-in hand-holding. The concept is easy. The feedback is rich.

However, many high-potential or highly creative individuals resent the simple all-or-nothing interface. Companies like WILL Interactive have advanced the genre to handle more complex moral situations, and a few of their products, unlike most other examples of the genre, are also appropriate for higher-level employees.

The sweet spot for branching stories may be as great prereading.

Genre 4: Interactive Spreadsheets

The fourth established genre of educational simulation is the interactive spreadsheet. If branching stories are easy, interactive spreadsheets are challenging

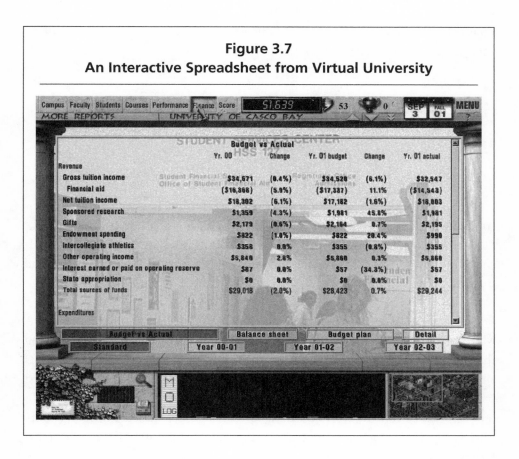

Figure 3.7
An Interactive Spreadsheet from Virtual University

(Figure 3.7 is an example). Whereas branching stories are self-contained, allowing instructors plenty of time for Facebook, interactive spreadsheets almost always need the hands-on guidance of a coach.

Born out of business schools (thanks, really), interactive spreadsheets are an educational simulation genre in which, depending on who is saying it, either (a) students gain business acumen and master complex interwoven system dynamics as they take charge of a fictitious organization, or (b) students typically try to affect three or four core metrics indirectly and over time by allocating finite resources along competing categories over a series of turns/intervals. Regardless, students get feedback on their decisions through graphs and charts after each interval.

The entire sim might continue for between two and fifteen intervals, with later turns involving more complexity and options. For example, the head of a research organization might try to optimize the variables of "great scientists retained," "patents earned," and "revenue" by allocating his or her time during the course of each week between

- recruiting,
- improving working conditions,
- allocating time of scientists,
- doing research, and
- engaging corporations or universities.

Interactive spreadsheets are often deployed in a multiplayer or team-based environment, with significant competition between learners, and often with a coach/facilitator to help everyone along. In this kind of environment, interactive spreadsheets are often the cornerstones of multiday units to build shared knowledge and understanding.

Genre 5: Practiceware

More meta-genre than genre, practiceware is a type of educational simulation that encourages participants to repeat actions in high-fidelity real-time, often 3-D situations until the skills become natural in the real-world counterpart. The first practiceware genre was the flight simulator, used for training pilots.

The practiceware interface constantly presents participants with five to twenty different actions, aligned with real-world options, many of which require mastery of split-second timing (when to do an action) and magnitude (how hard to do an action).

Practiceware can also model complex "internal" systems that are affected by participant actions, which in turn produce the results. Practiceware is used for learning goals that include implicit knowledge and can be a significant piece of a mastery level program.

Practiceware has at least some of the production attributes of a complex game. Its typically high development cost makes it more efficient for most organizations to buy it off the shelf or configured rather than built from scratch or even customized.

Genre 6: Minigames

The final popular genre of simulations is the minigame. Minigames, also called *casual games* or *micro games*, are easy to access, most often Adobe Flash–based, and require between five and twenty minutes of student engagement. Minigames may look superficially like frame games, but they embody the philosophy of practiceware. A minigame focuses on actions, systems, and results, although in a more abstract way than a more detailed simulation.

Minigames are both fun—because of their quick gameplay, often bouncy music, and appealing graphics—and educational. And with their relatively low development cost, they are actually doable for many organizations.

In one example, *Robo Rush* from the Acton School of Business, students play an entrepreneur through three phases. In phase 1, they go door to door selling robots (which they then have to actually build), negotiating with potential customers both to understand the demands of the marketplace and to find the most profitable segments.

In phase 2, the entrepreneur sets up shop and hires staff. In phase 3, the entrepreneur commits to a market segment through making long-term investments in factories and other infrastructure. Throughout the sim, the student-entrepreneurs meet with their accountant and are told how they are doing and what big choices they have to make. The total minigame takes students about one hour to run through. (Figure 3.8 shows three screens from *Robo Rush*.)

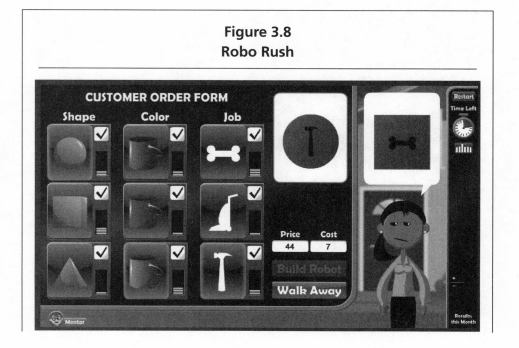

**Figure 3.8
Robo Rush**

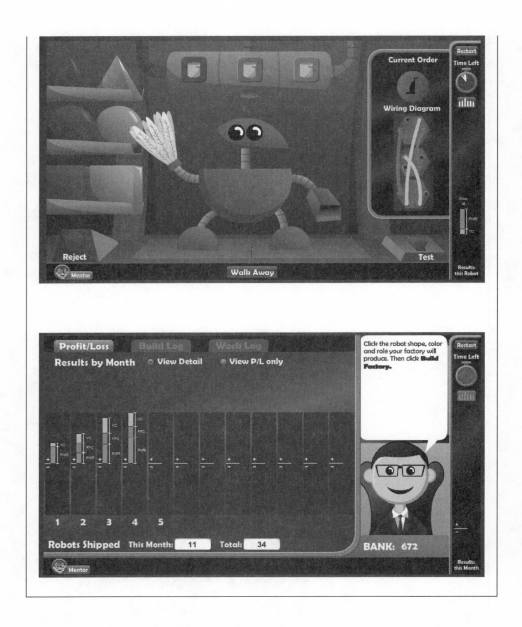

Minigames are perfect when there are a few skills or activities that need repetition and practice to be able to apply well, or there is some counterintuitive system in place or some new set of results desired.

FOUR CONCLUDING THOUGHTS

First, these genres are all approximate, and plenty of innovators will mix and match. Second, stand-alone sims have pioneered methodologies and structures that virtual-world-based sims might do well to copy, at least at first. Third, just because an organization has access to a virtual world does not mean it gets good sims for free. It has to build it out. And fourth, sim content has its own set of grammar and rules. The process of building out a sim from class notes is not straightforward at all, nor is going from "learning to know" to "learning to do." It is a new experience and has to be appreciated for a different approach.

Highly Interactive Content from the Students' and the Instructor's Perspective

Games, simulations, and virtual worlds represent a fundamentally different approach from traditional linear material. In the last chapter, we looked at how this interactive approach affects content. Now we will explore how it affects the fundamental learner experience.

DIFFERENT CULTURE, DIFFERENT RULES

Among the more obvious differences between highly interactive virtual environments and traditional classrooms are the new culture and social rules. These initially throw newcomers, but they represent a fairly minor shift in the overall student experience. Here are just two examples.

Synchronous Conversations

In contrast to a traditional lecture, in *Second Life*'s culture it is acceptable, and maybe even preferable, for people in the audience to chat with each other while a speaker is talking. (Increasingly, virtual classroom sessions have also embraced this meme.) While you might be talking to a hundred students, they are simultaneously talking to each other through the chat backchannel. More than a few instructors have found this distracting, and far too few instructors use this feature to adapt their own presentations.

So is it chaos? No, there still are rules of etiquette, if slightly different. For example, it is rude to chat and have a text conversation that is not about the topic at hand. Likewise, audience members, given the value of screen real estate, want to be careful about their noise-to-signal ratio, making sure comments are not only relevant but also fairly succinct. An example of bad manners is to keep typing your question when it is not immediately responded to. Another example is two people going back and forth on a single issue, monopolizing the conversation. When progress is no longer made, the conversation is best taken off-line. What other people often type in that situation is "get a room!"

This cultural attribute will get even more complicated. A future feature of many virtual environments is *threaded conversations*. Currently, a group can either all talk together or individual members can talk to other individual members. But eventually it will be possible for a group of colluding co-located people to be discussing four or five topics and to listen to and participate in different threads whenever they want to.

Making Emotional States Explicit

A second example of a new cultural attribute is worth noting: as people spend more time in virtual worlds, they learn to make their emotional states explicit. They do this not only through selecting animations for their avatars, but experienced virtual world inhabitants also often add comments about emotional states enclosed in asterisks, such as "That was a good point *smiles*" or "I'll see you later! *waves*"

LEARNING TO LOVE FRUSTRATION AND ANTICIPATE RESOLUTION

Adopting highly interactive virtual environments requires a more profound shift than just new communications strategies and etiquette. Much more. For a student of a simulation, engaging a sim itself is significantly different from using other types of formal learning programs. To fully appreciate this, we should zoom out and examine authentic learning, not classroom or book learning.

Here is a basic observation (clears throat): during the course of most transitions (from getting into a great school to moving to a better apartment), things get worse before they get better, even when the transition is sought after and desired. Intellectually, new clarity only follows frustration. New power comes from not being able to do things the way you have in the past. So it makes sense, and is even necessary, that a moment of learning is marked first by being frustrated at not being able to do something that we want to do and then resolving that frustration.

Consider your own experiences. When you learned to ride a bike, swim, play the trombone, or speak a foreign language, the process was most likely uneven, filled with lows and highs, frustrations and resolutions.

- There are moments when any learner wants to give up. We get mad. We blame the tools. We revise our desire to learn the subject matter. We envy people who work in toll booths. Some people quit.

- Then there is the "Aha!" moment when everything starts clicking together. We feel great. We look at ourselves in the mirror and smile. We charge on.

- The exaltation is then followed by another, more interesting frustration, and the cycle continues and our capabilities increase.

In authentic learning, the *frustration-resolution* pairing is the sensation of new mental muscle forming. When experiencing these situations formally, if asked, we have difficulty summing up, to ourselves and to others, what we learned. Words just trivialize the learning. But what was learned sticks with us. Hence we remember riding a bike forever, while forgetting what year the Magna Carta was signed five seconds before we need to write it on the test.

Sims, and educational simulations in particular, only minimally smooth out these peaks and valleys of real learning. Rather, they compress them and make them more predictable.

Despite this, when a student hits a valley of frustration, this can present a problem of expectations for the simulation coach or sponsor. Some students literally think the simulation is broken. When assured that it is not, they will think the simulation is just badly designed. Then they blame their teammates and the coach before they blame themselves. There is a tacit but predictable "threshold to quit" for different end-learners; if the experience dips below the threshold, the learner will opt out of the course with a negative bias.

Factors that raise the threshold to quit (making quitting more likely) include the following:

- The student is "evaluating" or "surveying" the material.

- The program has little support.

- The expectations for the sim experience have been poorly set up.

These factors lower the threshold (making quitting less likely):

- The course has a live coach/facilitator.
- The students understand that they really need the content.
- The program has a lot of credibility or good "buzz."

Frustration is a problem even in face-to-face simulations. But in online environments, where students tend to fret more in their isolation, it can derail the learning process. Therefore teaching someone to learn from a simulation often requires re-teaching them what it means to learn. The series of frustrations and resolutions needs to be foreshadowed and predicted. Getting students to learn to anticipate and love frustration, even to seek it out, is the essence of getting them to learn from interactive experience. Frustration will still sneak up on them even if they're prepared.

One of the oldest pieces of advice is still the best: if you're stuck on a problem, sleep on it. It is amazing how effective the subconscious is for working through tough problems as long as the student understands them before going to sleep. This does require the instructor to at least make sure that students don't procrastinate or cram.

WHEN THE MOST VALUABLE THING FOR A COACH TO DO IS NOTHING

Just as the role of students has to evolve to better embrace frustration, so too must the role of the traditional instructor evolve to embrace coaching. For clarity's sake, a coach is a human (or an avatar in some pre-scripted situations) that helps participants make the most of an experience, in a way that breaks the fourth wall of any virtual situation.

The specifics of this role change depending on what phase of the simulation deployment a student is in. A coach must

- initially present some background material (often through lectures),
- pace the individual student or group during the experience, sometimes forcing different approaches,
- conduct After Action Reviews, and sometimes even
- present and interpret pre- and post-course 360 review results or other long-term coaching for more intensive formal learning programs.

The constant dance of a coach is not to solve the users' frustrations but to help the users solve the frustrations themselves. Truly, a better model for an instructor using a simulation is a soccer coach rather than a teacher in a classroom.

One final question is, how much do instructors need to know to be good coaches? How much do they have to prepare? There is a range of answers. Some people believe that a professor should know the simulation better than any student before using it. Other professors have a broader approach—as long as they know some basics, they can rely on the simulation to do most of the teaching itself. Coaches are often the face to the students of a program, taking on technical support, scheduling, and logistical issues as well. Other students in the role of buddies can temporarily take on the role of one-on-one coach.

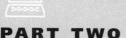

PART TWO

Choosing and Using a Highly Interactive Virtual Environment

Identifying the Right Approach for the Right Need

The biggest and most important confusion in curricula design is not, as we discussed in Part I, how an educational simulation is different from a virtual world. The biggest confusion is between when to use highly interactive content and when to use traditional content, such as lectures, tests, and reading and writing assignments. This chapter will identify areas in curricula and classes for which Highly Interactive Virtual Environments are natural fits.

To make this conversation easier, let's stipulate that highly interactive approaches are harder to build and use than linear content. (By the way, that will change in the next few years, as students increasingly become authors of content as well as consumers, which we are already seeing in some virtual worlds.) Pragmatically, this means when highly interactive approaches and linear content are equally well suited for a learning or other objective, we should use linear content.

Finally, this chapter has the conceit that instructors begin with a need and then fill that need with the right solution of virtual world, game, or educational simulation. From my own experience, most instructors instead want to implement some highly interactive virtual environment and then use the following reasons as rationale. (To which I say, "Fair enough!" The reasons can work either way.)

WHY USE DISTANCE LEARNING PROGRAMS AT ALL?

Before we get started on when to use various specific interactive approaches, it is worth noting briefly the key affordances of distance learning programs in general. Why? A broader goal of using interactive content will be to increase the existing benefits and take advantage of the new infrastructures they require while mitigating corresponding negatives.

Given that, one of the most critical advantages of distant learning programs is nearly universally accessible education. Assuming a computer and Internet access, people all over the world can access virtual classrooms without leaving their job or their community and without the significant transportation costs and dislocation costs involved in traditional education.

Distance learning has tangential benefits beyond student attendance and some green benefits: classes can access talent or even just plain folk that they could not access otherwise. For example, because it will take only an hour rather than a day, a guest speaker might agree to present to a class in a virtual world but not be willing to come in person. (I used to say that I would speak on my favorite topics for free and that the speaking fees were to cover the misery of travel.) If you are discussing the cold war, for example, you can bring in a professor from Russia to talk about it from an alternative perspective.

Another sine qua non of distance learning programs is that all students spend their class time in front of a computer using a common environment (such as virtual classroom tools, Flash, or *Protosphere*). This is in contrast to the often computationally heterogeneous environments of face-to-face classrooms. Highly interactive virtual environments are a logical extension to distributed learning, rather than something completely different.

However, there are downsides. In virtual environments, students can feel disconnected from each other and the instructor. In the corporate world in the 1970s and 1980s, employees used to joke that IBM stood for "I've been moved," referring the computer giant's tendency to require employees to relocate. Now employees joke instead that, due to the proliferation of virtual work, IBM should stand for "I'm by myself."

Another downside is that online students do not have physical access to facilities, including classrooms, student centers, and labs. Further, online content can be dull and flat; "death by PowerPoint" has been not only refined in many online programs but weaponized to nearly military specifications.

WHEN TO USE HIGHLY INTERACTIVE CONTENT

With the preceding advantages and downsides as context, here are some key reasons to consider highly interactive content (starting with virtual worlds, then games, and finally educational simulations). These answers will overlap.

To Create a Sense of Presence, Use Virtual Worlds

An early and central value of virtual worlds is that they provide a sense of presence. This can have a physical benefit, such as showing a three-dimensional model of a building or a super-sized model of a squid. But this sense of presence also has a greater emotional and social impact. Unlike with traditional virtual classroom infrastructures, students in a virtual world feel as if they are physically near other people, not just viewing the same artifacts.

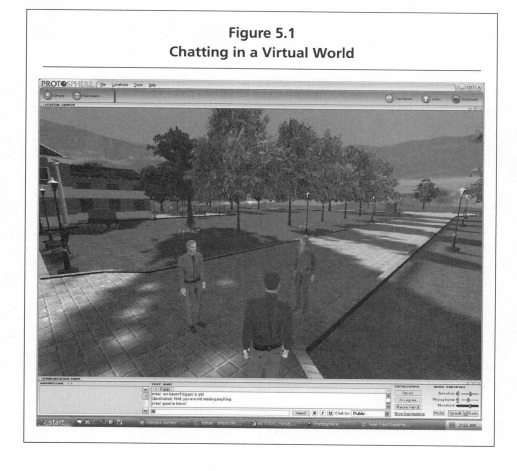

Figure 5.1
Chatting in a Virtual World

Robert Bloomfield, creator in 2007 of the virtual world talk show *Metanomics* (and professor of management and accounting at Cornell University's Johnson Graduate School of Management), notes that anyone can quickly observe the change in behaviors for themselves. As students and instructors get more comfortable in virtual places like *Second Life*, they change the way that they behave. Their on-screen avatar (their representation in the virtual world) demonstrates similar patterns to their "meat body" on a physical campus. These changes include some basic behaviors, like pacing when nervous, and even how they move their arms or their face.

Further, by the third or fourth session, students might arrive fifteen minutes early and talk among themselves much as they would before a face-to-face class. They may kibitz about movies or politics or other classes. After the session, students are likely to hang around and maybe walk together to some other location and continue class discussions (thus the more effective classrooms in a virtual world include access to social rooms). This behavior is in contrast to the "one minute before login" that most people use for virtual classroom tools, with the immediate drop-off when done.

The sense of presence can also extend beyond distance learning to purely social situations and to field trips. Organizations may throw large fund-raisers or get-togethers in virtual worlds. Meanwhile, classes can visit virtual facilities (that may be doing real work) more efficiently than in the physical world.

To Easily Access Diverse Real-World Communities, Use Virtual Worlds

Vibrant virtual worlds can provide access to real, organic communities, as well as individual experts. For example if you were learning to speak French, you could find on *Second Life* a community of people currently living in France speaking French typically about current events or some other topic of cultural interest.

To Increase Student Engagement, Use Games

Essentially, games (in the broadest sense, including not only class games and group challenges but also sims, such as serious games and educational simulations, and both stand-alone or in virtual worlds) should be used when students need to be more engaged than they are. When students are not expressing interest in the content or demonstrating only rote learning, introducing interactive content can attract and engage them. It can be light and fun, or it can be deep and challenging. Students will be grateful.

The use of games is scalable and recursive. If a semester-long course is failing to generate much conversation or comprehension, then a relatively complicated simulation may add depth. But all classes have natural low spots, often one or two per hour, says InSync Training's Kassy LaBorie. A quick five-minute class game can reinvigorate a sagging community especially after a linear lecture or even after a complicated turn with an intense educational simulation.

To Provide Access to Labs and Props, Use Stand-Alone Sims or Sims in Virtual Worlds

One use of interactive environments, and perhaps the simplest argument to make for them, is to enable access to labs. For example, a traditional chemistry, physics, or engineering class may rely on labs in the meat world. But the equivalent online class can use virtual models that have the same characteristics. These labs and props can be stand-alone, as in Flash (see Figure 5.2), or built into a virtual world environment.

In fact, given how many real tools are expensive, dangerous, finicky, inaccessible, or fragile, virtual tools can give students experience with more tools than in a traditional class. Virtual tools can be not only cheaper but also better, with the ability to do such things as provide views into their inner workings.

Students can also build labs in some virtual environments, not just participate in them. As we will discuss in the assessment chapter (Chapter 10), this significantly changes the learning goal, for both better and worse.

To Increase Depth of Knowledge, Use Educational Simulations or Environments, Either Stand-Alone or in Virtual Worlds

If students need a deeper and richer knowledge base, one in which they can improvise to meet a variety of surprise situations, simulations work well. The more students need to intellectually understand a topic, the less sufficient are simple rules and processes. Consequently, interactive labs can be used in nontraditional areas, such as mathematical concepts, weather, and historical locations or economies, and even in interpersonal areas.

Simulations are appropriate when the content is inherently dynamic (in contrast to the timelines or inner monologues stressed by linear content).

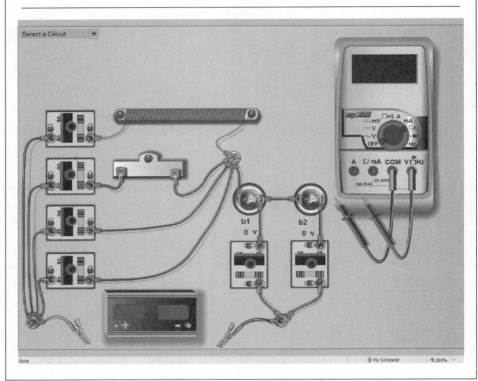

Figure 5.2
An Adobe Flash version of engineering tools with complete fidelity cheaply replaces the real thing, so instructors do not have to use physical examples.

Content is dynamic when it is naturally made up of the three layers we talked about with flight simulators (Chapter 1):

- *actions* (which transfers to the interface of the sim),
- *results* (where there is a goal to be accomplished), and
- one or more *systems* that connect the two.

A simulation is a good choice if students are not understanding the content or if the content has become so abstracted that it does not meet the original learning intent. Where the content is based on mathematical relationships (even if students never see the numbers directly), stand-alone simulations will work better. Where the content is based on multiplayer team-based interactions, virtual worlds will often serve as a better environment.

Where Using the Content Is Critical, Choose Educational Simulations, Either Stand-Alone or in Virtual Worlds

One should always use educational simulations (and not serious games) when the successful application of the content is critical—as it is with pilots, nuclear power operators, and Wall Street traders. Where failure is not an option, and if the situation can be simulated, instructors will probably already be using simulators.

Educational simulations should also be used when content is meant to be applied beyond the classroom but currently is not. For example, if an organizational behavior class is striving to drive real changes in the behavior of the students once they leave the classroom but is failing, then simulations might be a good choice.

This need can be determined by simply interviewing students six months after content has been delivered. One can also survey instructors by asking them what existing programs are critical from a content perspective but ineffective from a delivery perspective?

Try Using HIVEs That Are Already Available

This last point of the "when should highly interactive learning be used" checklist is perhaps the least satisfying. Professors who cannot build their own simulations, or hire someone to do it, must use simulations that already exist. Given the relative paucity of existing simulations (at least compared to text books), an appropriate one may not be available.

COSTS ASSOCIATED WITH HIVES

One of the critical factors in choosing if, when, and how to use a HIVE, and which one to use, is cost. Cost can be influenced by a variety of factors, including

- the complexity of the game or simulation,
- the length,
- whether it is an off-the-shelf product or must be custom-made or modified to fit an instructor's learning goals, and
- whether coaching and support fees are included in the price.

Table 5.1
Costs of HIVE Formats

	Off-the-the shelf (price per user)			Custom (price per site license)		
	Short (>10 min.)	Medium (10–30 min.)	Long (30 minutes– 2+ hours)	Short (>10 min.)	Medium (10–30 min.)	Long (30 minutes– 2+ hours)
Branching story	$30	$100	$500	$30,000	$50.000	$500.000
Interactive spreadsheet	$30**	$100**	$500**	$30,000**	$50,000**	$500,000**
Minigame	free	free	free	$10,000	$15,000	$40,000
Virtual lab	$10	$30	$100	$30,000	$75,000	$150,000
Practiceware	$100	$400	$1,000	$100,000	$500,000	$1 million

* plus cost of facilitation
** including cost of facilitation

Table 5.1 shows some general costs associated with the various HIVE formats. These are broad estimates, from sampling that I have done in three different worlds, academic, corporate, and military. Academic pricing for bulk orders and for off-the-shelf products can be as low as one-tenth of these numbers. Academic orders for custom work can be offset by instructors preparing as much of the material as they can.

The cost of accessing a virtual world is a little more interesting. Universities have three initial options to hold classes on *Second Life*: they can buy a little piece of land on the mainland, rent from other people, or buy an island (which is, under the covers, buying a server).

Buying an island gives the university the most control, so it is often the path of choice. Taking advantage of a significant academic discount, schools typically pay a one-time fee of $3,000 and then about $200 dollars a month. Compared to a virtual classroom tool, this is a little less expensive.

Students and teachers can then get on the island and even set up their own avatar for free. About fifty to one hundred avatars can occupy an island at a time. Of course, just having the property is not enough. Universities then have to construct their own structures. However, a lot of colleges buy an island and get students to build the buildings for them.

Doing the Prep Work

As with painting a room or invading a foreign country, using simulations takes a lot of prep work, some of it tedious. This chapter will detail the steps to prepare for using highly interactive environments, including evaluating options, selecting one, learning about it, and preparing support material for it. Here are the key steps.

CONNECT WITH OTHER INTERESTED PROFESSIONALS

Professors who are interested in using HIVEs should first try to connect with the people at the leading edge of this technology. They should not reinvent the wheel. Because distributed educational models allow for easy access, interested instructors should log hours watching other people do what they want to.

If the area of interest is *Second Life*, they should explore *Second Life* in their free time, attend public events, and hang out and chat with various subject matter experts. There are many classes in *Second Life* today, and many more instructors interested in exploring best practices this area. The International Society of Technology Educators (ISTE), as one example, has a big educator presence in Second Life.

Professors who are interested in games should attend a few sessions of colleagues using games. Watching an educational simulation deployment may take a bit longer, but it is well worth the investment.

ACCESS THE CONTENT

Accessing Virtual Worlds

***Second Life* is still the standard** The various virtual worlds are different from each other, not only in community but also in cost, technology approach, quality of experiences, and even level of security. Their respective merits should (in theory) be compared when considering them for adoption. For example, as with stand-alone sims, virtual worlds can be downloadable on PCs and/or Macs or Web deployed.

Although there are credible alternatives such as Forterra Olive, ProtonMedia's *ProtoSphere* (the choice of Duke University's Fuque School of Business, in part, according to some, because students could not take off their clothes), *Open Croquet, Sun Wonderland,* and *Active Worlds,* many researchers and even practitioners use *Second Life* as being synonymous to all virtual worlds. The default platform is still *Second Life,* and it likely will be during the foreseeable future. Right now, there are quite a few (dozens? hundreds? thousands? billions and billions? it depends on how you count) virtual worlds out there. These are environments that have both a visual sense of space (often three-dimensional) and a lot of real people populating them.

They go by a lot of names. The technical name is Massively Multiplayer Online Environments (MMOs), which includes Massively Multiplayer Online Role-Playing Games (MMORPGs). *Massively multiplayer* implies a sense of persistence—the world is always on. Depending on your own interests, either *World of Warcraft* or *Second Life* is an example.

Using highly interactive virtual environments with students obviously means gaining access or building them. Here are the best ways to do it.

Some persistent virtual worlds, the so-called meta-verses, are capable of concurrently hosting hundreds (and often thousands, or tens of thousands) of real people, and participants can enter and exit in an open-ended manner. Once "in world," participants, often represented as people-like avatars, can meaningfully interact (by voice over internet protocols [VOIP], instant messaging, performing tasks/objectives/goal/missions, trading, and creating artifacts) with each other and the environment.

Among the reasons for its popularity:

- *Second Life,* unlike the alternatives, has reached the critical mass (the number of users) necessary for long-term growth. This creates stability, variety, and a variety of communities, as well a situation where *Second Life* is sucking up most of the oxygen in the space.

- *Second Life,* while not available in a pure Web form such as Google's erstwhile virtual world *Lively* was, is available for both Macs and PCs. It has to be downloaded and installed, but that results in a richer experience than Web-only models.

- Technically, *Second Life* allows participants to move seamlessly between servers, increasing the size of the world dramatically (although interacting groups should be less than one hundred and ideally less than fifty).

But the more important advantage might be that *Second Life* also has its own integrated internal toolset for animations and graphics. Amateur authors can quickly create (or increasingly "buy" in the dynamic economy and then modify) a variety of rich content. This ability to build is critical. For an instructor or institution, entire facilities can be built in a few weeks. More importantly, this year's students can build and improve labs for next year's. The bad news, however, is that these tools are specific to *Second Life*; institutions cannot leverage the hundreds of thousands of *3D Max, Maya,* or *Poser* authors out there, for example, to create *Second Life* environments and objects. Also, in contrast to *Second Life*, ProtonMedia is built on the Microsoft stack, so it is completely compatible with other tools, such as *SharePoint*.

Still, *Second Life* may just be the emerging content aggregator of all multimedia, at least according to Randy Hinrichs, former Group Operations Manager at Microsoft's Advanced Strategies Group and now CEO of 2b3d. *Second Life* can increasingly integrate wikis and blogs and RSS feeds, video and audio, even 3-D animations and sets.

First, use others' *Second Life* classes   Another advantage is that professors can also approach *Second Life* cautiously. *Second Life* makes money not by allowing an individual to go "in world" (which is free) but by selling virtual real estate. So download the *Second Life* application for free, create an avatar, and explore. Students can as well.

Further, when an institution needs a presence in *Second Life*, the first instinct is often to buy land (in the form of an island) and build a three-dimension facility. However, organizations should focus first on running great events, rather than spending a lot of money on the perfect classroom or classroom environments or island.

The truth is that there are a lot of empty classrooms and other workspaces in *Second Life*. (In fact there are a lot of entire ghost towns.) So find an institution that is interested in building up traffic, schedule time, and have your classes meet there initially.

(Appropriately for some, *World of Warcraft* is free for a trial period, often long enough for classroom engagement, but not enough to get to Level 70.)

Accessing Stand-Alone Sims

The question of finding the right stand-alone sim, including educational simulations and games, is a bit more nuanced than either virtual world or game. It is important to consider where stand-alone sims academic classes come from. There are several kinds of sources, each with its own trade-offs (for example, fairly or unfairly, a sim's origin and source affect how and if students are asked to pay for it directly):

Commercial off-the-shelf games   For some lucky professors and students, computer games built for entertainment and bought through retail channels provide a deep enough and curriculum-aligned enough experience.

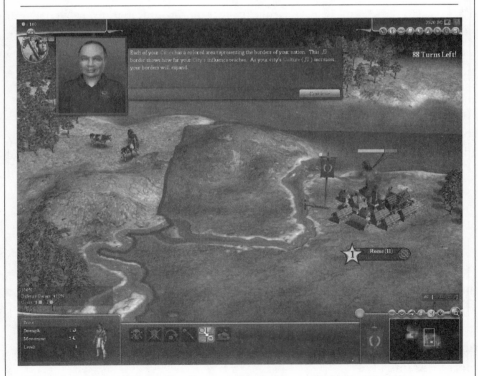

Figure 6.1
A Screen Shot from *Civilization IV*

Sid Meier's Civilization IV Screen Shot Courtesy of Firaxis Games and Take-Two Interactive Software, Inc.

The two most famous are the *Civilization* and *SimCity* series. The pros are reasonable per-student costs (around $40), very high production values and tutorials, and at least some element of fun built in. They are fairly open-ended as well so professors can assign goals and challenges aligned to class objectives. The biggest con is that only a few such games exist. Further, both deans and parents can be uncomfortable having the students spend class time playing off-the-shelf games (and really, don't push it and try to use *Maus* as the textbook for the same class using *Civilization*, no matter how much history is on your side). These games can also be awkward to install, requiring 3-D cards and updated drivers. There are many published "cheat codes" available. And students typically directly bear the cost of their purchase in academic environments.

Obviously, computer games were not built to be accurate. But as Richard N. Van Eck, associate professor and graduate director of Instructional Design and Technology at the University of North Dakota, points out, "errors and inaccuracies are in fact teachable moments." Asking students to find inaccuracies and then document and defend their statements can be the best of all worlds.

Free sims from foundations, causes, or corporations   A lot of free, typically Adobe Flash–based sims have been created in the last few years by various organizations. They represent some of the most successful and innovative examples of serious games including Cisco's *Binary Numbers* and American Public Media's *Budget Hero*.

If they fit, they can be perfect. The pros are that they are free and typically easy to access. The cons are that they are short, often shallow, and often editorially skewed. Some, although not these examples, represent a position that could easily be wrong or even offensive (blatant stereotypes in sims really get people mad). Further, a sim that is interesting and relevant may not be around next week if the sponsor changes its mind or even gets sued.

Off-the-shelf or custom vendor-supplied educational simulations   Some vendors sell prepackaged off-the-shelf simulations. The pros are numerous. They tend to be rich and detailed educational experiences. They have technical support. They also have instructional support—notes for how to use them in a classroom environment. They may have gone through several generations of modifications. And often the best supporting documentation has been rigorously gathered from other users. The cons are that the licensing is often restrictive and the costs tend

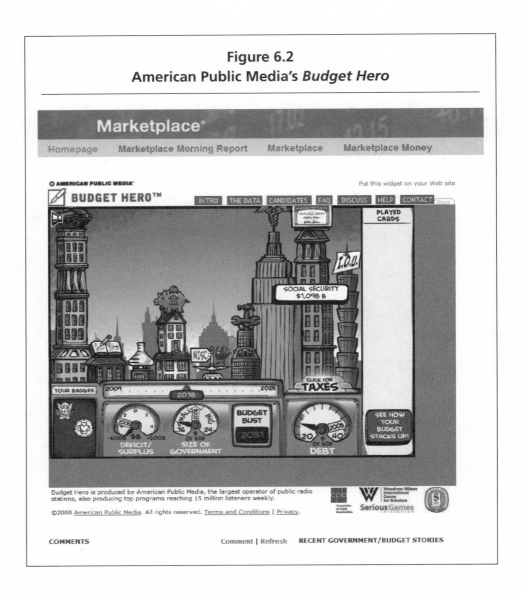

Figure 6.2
American Public Media's *Budget Hero*

to be three or four times as much as a computer game. Students typically directly bear this cost.

Many off-the-shelf educational simulations have configurable attributes, including custom configurations for different environments such as undergraduate, graduate, and executive education, as well as corporate use. Some simulations even provide access to variables in the models so that professors can customize the systems to align with their own curricula.

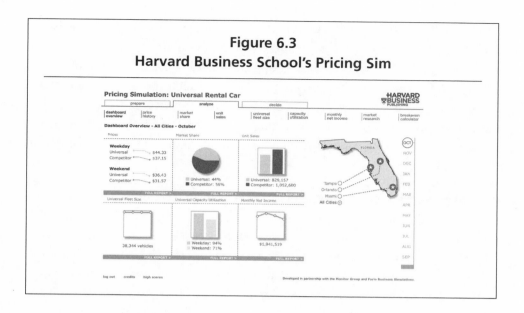

Figure 6.3
Harvard Business School's Pricing Sim

The supporting manuals for off-the-shelf educational simulations are often the best way for a professor to peek under the covers and learn more about it. Therefore the first step in piloting is to review the printed material.

Internal development group   Some institutions have a staff of people (usually between one and twenty) who are dedicated to building simulations to support internal classes. The good news is that these people are focused, have the requisite skills, and are aligned with the goals of the institution. Once built, the content can most likely be infinitely reused and shared. The cons are that the resulting experiences are often dry have an odd, if any, sense of humor, are buggy, hard to update, and take three or four times longer to build than expected. These internal development groups predictably fight with the subject matter experts (the professors), from whom they have to draw content, over time and ownership. Who funds these groups is also up for grabs from budget cycle to budget cycle, sometimes minimizing long-term continuity.

One other alternative for internal development is to use grad students or gaming students. They can be very useful references, and the price is right. Regardless, despite these rather harrowing and possibly Shakespearean conflicts of interest, look for this internal development trend to continue to grow.

Modified off-the-shelf computer games   Some professors modify existing off-the-shelf computer games, including graphics, settings, sometimes interfaces, and goals, to make them appropriate for their class. These bundles of changes are called *mods*. The pro is that for not much money, professors can access very rich environments. The cons are that student still have to buy the original computer game, and compromises often have had to be made in order to shoehorn the changes into the computer game, resulting in a suboptimal or even unstable experience.

Professor-created simulations   We are seeing an explosion of technology-savvy academic hobbyists creating simulations to support their class, developed in their free time. (It was professor hobbyists who, decades ago, created the thriving educational simulation genre of *interactive spreadsheets*.) The pros are that these tend to be perfectly aligned with content and are deep and nuanced. They can also be freely shared. The cons are that the simulations are often makeshift, with kludgy interfaces. They also tend to be more like labs than finished sims. Knowledge of how they were built, the assumptions that were made, and how to best use them tends not to get recorded.

It is worth noting the pricing models for sims one more time. Imagine that the cost of accessing a thousand units of a sim is $50,000. If the sim is structured to be sold per seat, often by an external vendor, then each student will typically have to pay for access, as they would for a textbook. But if the cost is paid in a lump sum or in salaries, it tends to be the department that picks up the tab. Just as with dating, this part of life is hugely unfair. But unlike with dating, at least this is predictable.

Ten Off-the-Shelf Single-Player Games and Educational Simulations

The first three are commercial off-the-shelf (COTS) computer games. They all fall into the broad category of "God games."

1. Sid Meier's *Civilization* series by Firaxis (http://www.firaxis.com/) for history and social sciences.

2. *SimCity* series by Electronic Arts (http://simcity.ea.com/play/simcity_classic.php and http://simcity.ea.com/index.php) for urban planning and social psychology.

3. *Age of Empires* series by Microsoft (www.microsoft.com/games/empires) for history.

The next five are specialized.

4. *Making History* (http://www.making-history.com/) for history.

5. *Skytech* by ExperiencePoint (http://www.experiencepoint.com/sims/SkyTech) for high-level business skills.

6. *Capstone* Business Simulation (http://www.capsim.com/) for high-level business skills.

7. *Virtual Leader* (and *VLeader*) (http://www.simulearn.net/) for first-person leadership, organizational behavior, and interpersonal skills.

8. *Virtual University* (www.virtual-u.org/index.php) for university management and economics.

The last two are also COTS games, focusing on economics. Although they are more common in high school curricula, they are used in undergraduate programs as well.

9. *Zoo Tycoon* by Microsoft (www.microsoft.com/games/pc/zootycoon2.aspx) for planning and economics.

10. *Roller Coaster Tycoon* by Chris Sawyer Games and Atari (www.atari.com/rollercoastertycoon) for planning and economics.

INFRASTRUCTURE SELECTION CRITERIA

Regardless of from where a highly interactive virtual environment is accessed, it has to have the right attributes to be accessed and efficiently used. These criteria can filter out external offerings or guide the development of internal ones. Here are some of the most important from an infrastructure perspective.

Technology Accessible by Most Students

A virtual environment must be able to run on the technology platform used by at least 90 percent of the students. ("Hmm," you may be thinking. "90 percent, not 100 percent. Intriguing, passionate, yet somehow cruel.") In most cases, the few students with the most outdated technology should not drag down the richness of the experience for the rest of the class. Instead, they should figure out how to access it or even acquire better technology on their own. When a student asked how to access six-year-old technology, one instructor's canned response was "Make a friend." While this response may seem unfair to such students, we know that as technology improves and access becomes more affordable, this will become less of a challenge. It is important to balance the needs of the students with the learning opportunities provided by using a richer HIVE.

At a broad level, the three choices are Apple/MAC, PC, or web-deployed. Web-deployed might break between Adobe Flash and HTML, and Adobe Flash doesn't currently run on Apple iPhone or iPod Touch. Then, there may be hardware considerations including speed of processors, the availability and power of graphic cards and sound, and (less winnowing) browser type. Finally there is network speed.

Typically in a distributed environment, the specifics of the students' infrastructure is pretty well known, or even predetermined by other factors or requirements. One can play it safe and just dovetail with user requirements of the other aspects of the online program, including the required common virtual classroom tool and course management system. However, one can perform a technology survey of an existing class if one wants to know for sure or decide mid-course if the students can handle a new HIVE

Further, there are often some configuration and software issues outside of the hardware itself. To help with this, some HIVE vendors include a customized technology test page. This is a Web page that diagnoses the users' computers and settings for compatibility of all of the technology, networking capabilities, and security access that is needed for the successful use of a sim. Before an instructor or student enters a simulation, he or she can go (or maybe be directed) to this page and find any problems.

Typically, the areas of interest for a test page or technology survey are

- the presence of Flash (or the newest version of Flash)
- ability to communicate with external servers (for instant messaging or multiplayer)
- screen size and resolution
- sound capability, such as presence of headphones, speakers, microphone (if needed), and sound levels

- newest graphic card, sound card, and DirectX drivers (if needed)
- graphic card memory size
- hard disk size
- up-to-date installed game and doesn't need any patches
- sufficiently defragged hard disk

A good technology test page may also provide solutions and workarounds, such as links to driver homepages (such as Flash), or launch an HTML instead of Flash versions of the program or communication tools.

In this age of smart phones (like iPhones), netbooks, and game consoles (like PlayStations and Xboxes), we will see more multiplatform environments. Until then, we have to make some choices.

Instructor Controls

Here is another infrastructure selection criterion. Some virtual environments give the instructor a centralized ability to control, or gate, the progress of students in the simulation. For example, an instructor might assign students to access only the preparation material and first practice level but not move on to the rest of the levels. If the right tools exist, an instructor could force that rather than just ask. Of course, reporting tools can give soft control—if students know that their foray into level 2 will be reported back to the instructor, they may decide not to do it if the instructor told them not to.

Selection of Classrooms in *Second Life*

If instructors are considering *Second Life*, they also have to make choices within the vast community. Which island should they assign? Which facilities should they adopt? Which vendor should they use to help? In fact, making the easy decision to adopt *Second Life* is increasingly just postponing the real choices about content, not avoiding them.

Increasingly, the most important attribute of virtual environments will be their ability to enable students to collaboratively build complex artifacts. But there is also the need to have students in more traditional classroom settings. Given that, classrooms in *Second Life* have some different requirements than in the real world.

There should be a way for students to interact with the instructor and the rest of the class, such as raising their hands or voting on various survey questions.

Some seats in some classrooms, for example, have interactive screens built in. Another point highlights the different physics of a virtual world: participants in *Second Life* can only see each other's text-based chats if they are no farther than about 20 meters apart. This means that individuals should be fairly close to each other for a common class, but if there are multiple groups, they should meet fairly far away from each other. Specifically, breakout groups should be quite far away from other breakout groups. Classrooms do not need roofs, as students may arrive via flying.

CONTENT SELECTION CRITERIA

The previous section discussed selection criteria for the infrastructure. But highly interactive virtual environments also include media and content. When material is structured (as sims in stand-alone or as locations and facilities in a virtual world) here are the criteria.

Curriculum Alignment

Obviously, the interactive content must cover some part of the curriculum. Now, you are probably thinking, that is a staggeringly obvious comment. Actually, as with going from a book to a movie, it gets a bit more interesting.

This overlap is hardly ever one-to-one, in both what is covered compared to a traditional curricula and how long it takes to cover it. Sims tend to go deep, so what can be covered broadly at linear level might take three or four times as long when practiced. Further, almost any learning through discovery takes longer than a presentation of findings. However, some virtual labs and other exercises can actually be completed in one quarter of the time compared to a traditional class.

Although the criteria of the fit into the curriculum is fairly forgiving (most adopters will accept a "good enough" answer), for some subjects, instructors want the content aligned down to the decimal point. In a pricing simulation, for example, the exact way price elasticity is handled can be the difference between adoption and rejection.

Instructor Support Materials

Ideally interactive content should come with some type of instructor manual, facilitator's guide, or other instructor support (which may be online and may be password protected). Certainly richer supporting content should tip the scale between two otherwise competitive sims. Typically, if a sim is from a third-party vendor, it should come with significant support material. If the community using the sim is large enough, there should be access to a forum where questions can be asked.

Here are some nice-to-have deliverables:

- *Slides and talking points:* fully usable and editable decks of slides, which with minimal formatting can be inserted into any class. This can include walk-throughs on how to install or access, use the interface, use any prepackaged self-evaluation tools, and submit results where necessary.

- *Details on the underlying system:* simulations are often made up of rules and equations. Which rules and any relative weighting should be included.

- *Technical support frequently asked questions:* a list of the top twenty technical problems, with answers, culled from past deployments.

- *Examples of best, typical, and worst plays:* either detailed screenshots and text or video clips showing a range of plays, with both annotations and analysis of actions.

- *Tips for debriefing:* a guide to how to debrief the simulation if necessary. Typically, soft skill simulations require two to three times more space in the manual dedicated to helping instructors with debriefing than more technical skills.

- *Cheat codes:* a list of keystrokes or other hidden ways for someone to "cheat" in the simulation, such as jump ahead, have unlimited resources, see equations or variables that are otherwise hidden, play any video clip, or see alternative paths.

- *The ability to drain gastric fluids:* Sorry. This entry belongs on a different list. Carry on.

- *Modding tips:* a list of places and examples where the simulation is easy to change.

- *Bibliography for the simulation:* the answer to the question, how did you come up with the content for the simulation?

- *Further reading:* a list of books and articles where an interested person can get more information on the content overview in the sim.

- *Examples of syllabi:* three or four examples of places in typical course outlines where other professors have used the sim. This material can typically be edited as well.

Harvard Business School Publishing's Denis Saulnier explains his philosophy for guides:

> They are meant to do two things. They are meant to be teaching notes, such as we use for case studies. There are often no right or wrong answers to the sims, so the guides list out the learning objectives, the most common and expected student outcomes, and ways of connecting them. We guard that content carefully and only give it out to authorized instructors (college faculty and corporate instructors, for example). But a second part of the guides are also the user's guide—akin to a software manual. This content should be, at least in theory, more readily available to anyone who's interested. But because they show so many screens from later on in the sim, we have to be careful in their distribution as well.

Some Form of Artifact

Curriculum alignment and ability to run in a given environment may be the two absolutes for selecting simulation-based content. But there are some other criteria as well.

When I was a cognitive science major at Brown University, my favorite professor had a funny complaint. He noted that when he and his biology colleague were both relatively unproductive after spending all day working in their labs, at least his biology colleague had a pile of dead animals to show for her work. Likewise, when I talked to Will Wright about his success with *The Sims*, he told me how important it was that players could share artifacts, including houses and pictures, with each other. These artifacts made them feel like they were not wasting their time for the hours they put into the game.

Both the designers of educational simulations and the people who select them must think about artifacts. What are the footprints left behind in the digital sand, both deliberately and inevitably? Some artifacts are fairly simple. Recorded grades and progress made are natural and traditional outputs of any learning program. But they are not enough.

Other artifacts can help a teacher or professor evaluate what the student did. They can include timelines or periodic screen snapshots. Such artifacts are important because when one instructor is supervising 20 or even 200 students at a distance, he or she cannot watch everyone in real time. Instructors need some kind of summary of actions taken.

Still other artifacts are more like *The Sims*. This gets closer to the social networking world. Players want to impress each other with their creativity. If they did something unique or surprising, they want to show off. One form of this is the high score. Posting this does increase engagement from the other students. In one academic deployment of SimuLearn's vLeader, teams of students carefully watched the highest score of other teams, and when breakthroughs were made, there was a flurry of activity from the competitive teams to try to beat them. As more creative approaches are captured and required by a simulation, the ability to share them with colleagues becomes ever more important.

At the simplest level, students can take screenshots, print, or e-mail information for credit. This can force an instructor to evaluate on the mercurial but critical area of aesthetics.

One of the earliest complaints against e-learning was how unsatisfying it was to finish a program. So it is critical to note that social networking structures and rewards may provide a better motivation for accomplishment than petty certificates or even instructors' pats on the head.

SELF-PACED/SINGLE PLAYER, ASYNCHRONOUS, OR SYNCHRONOUS

Affecting both infrastructure and content for any game (including sims) is the decision of self-paced/single player, asynchronous, or synchronous:

- *Self-paced/single player:* Students engage the game by themselves. *SimCity* is single player, as is a batting cage. Single player has the most flexibility, and it can enable nearly endless practicing, but is also the most limited.

- *Asynchronous:* Students engage the game with other people (either colleagues or opponents), but not at the same time. Students are necessarily dependent on each other. At times they will have to wait for other players to submit information before they can take certain actions, and other people will be waiting on them.

- *Synchronous:* Students engage the game at the exact same time as other students. While this is the most open-ended, it also has the most variability and requires the most work to schedule.

Some distance learning programs require that programs be asynchronous or even single player as part of their deployment and organizational philosophy. This can obviously be a deal killer for a synchronous program.

Single Player Compared to Multiplayer

Most people blur the line between single player and multiplayer sims. But when they do differentiate, they prefer multiplayer. This preference for multiplayer has several sources:

- There are great entertainment and social successes like *World of Warcraft* and *Second Life* which industry gurus/quacks love extolling.
- Multiplayer experiences feel real, are rich in interface, and are dynamic.
- Multiplayer environments are, in theory, reusable. They represent a capability and process, even an infrastructure, not just content.

But there are also huge limitations to multiplayer. In most current educational simulations and serious games (unlike MMORPGs), multiplayer sims share many characteristics of a classroom role-play:

- Everyone is on their best behavior. No one is going to tell another to "pound salt" as they might in the real world.
- People are reluctant to try risky new strategies.
- The logistics of setting them up is expensive and brittle.
- People can go through them once or twice, but then the players get bored.
- There is little consistency. Some people take their roles seriously, some do not. Friday afternoon role-plays are different than Monday at 10:00 a.m.
- There is little opportunity for rigorous After Action Reviews (or debriefings).
- They allow people to play out existing techniques and strategies, but not to predictably learn new ones or rigorously practice old ones.

Now admittedly, the live role-plays are often the best part of any classroom experience. They are usually staggeringly better than the lecture that surrounds them. The correct procedure, in a perfect world, is to first role-play in a single-player sim for exposure and practice and then to role-play in a multiplayer environment, which is more complex and open-ended.

How to Turn a Single-Player Sim into Multiplayer

Single-player sims can be made multiplayer in the following ways:

- Any sim that produces scores invites competition. Game players used to scratch their initials and their high scores onto the side of pinball machines, before game designers built it in as a feature starting with the coin-operated arcade game *Asteroids*. All that is needed is a validated repository and perhaps filtering by one's relevant community.
- Players can share artifacts with each other.
- Communities can form to debate best approaches or solutions to puzzles.

TRUST

A final criterion for selection is trust. Even at a place oozing with prestige like Wharton, the professors on the first day feel the need build credibility. They may refer to a graduate who is a current successful CEO. They may refer to well-known alums whom they taught personally.

So if Wharton has to establish its credibility, you can imagine the challenge with sims. Educational simulations must convince the player to work through the frustration, and serious games must earn a certain degree of trust. Trust can come from a perception of professionalism: the program behaves as it should, including loading; there are no spelling errors or other red flags. Other techniques that add credibility include prominently displayed logos and affiliations and statements of benefits.

Earning trust is the yin to level design's yang. To both ensure trust and reduce the need for it, good level design, or game mapping, pulls in the participants, slowly teaching them necessary skills and always moderating the amount of frustration to the appropriate level.

CONCLUSION: MIGHT VIRTUAL WORLDS BE THE UNIVERSAL INTERFACE TO (OTHER) SIMS?

The talk of future features in *Second Life* or other virtual worlds is interesting both because they may be coming and because they signify a slight problem today. One feature, already in experimentation today, could become a game changer. Let me zoom out a bit.

Figure 6.4
Playing the Sims while the Sims Are Playing a Game

There is this great moment in a couple of computer games where you, as a player, walking around a virtual world, stumble upon a classic 1980s-style coin-operated arcade game. This game within a game, or even a virtual world within a virtual world, provides a certain Matrix-esque experience, making you think about the nature of reality.

But I wonder if this technique will evolve into more than just a gimmick. Here are some premises:

- *Second Life* has gained tremendous interest as an environment for formal learning, including in academics, military, and corporations. This is in part because instructors are comfortable in this environment, as it is analogous to a traditional classroom in many ways.

- *Second Life* is not natively a great simulation environment, but it can be the most powerful when it interfaces beyond *Second Life*. For example, a corporation may hold a meeting in *Second Life* and use a "virtual" Polycom phone to call real people outside *Second Life*.

- Meanwhile, although virtual worlds present a single tool and interface for multiple purposes (meetings, prototyping, data visualization, classrooms, and social kibitzing), educational simulations may just be the opposite—with multiple forms (or genres) all serving the "single" purpose of formal learning. This can easily cause confusion among both instructors and students in terms of how to access and how to use educational simulations.

Given all the above, one can't help but wonder if, within a planning horizon, *Second Life* (or its successor in a few years) will actually become a universal interface to a diversity of deep educational simulations. Obviously this would require overcoming some significant interface and visual barriers today.

Integrating and Piloting

We have discussed identifying the right place for highly engaging learning, gaining some support, and finally procuring a highly interactive virtual environment. The final items in our predeployment checklist are technical support for students, chunking, and piloting. (I will leave the other items of swearing, praying, and furrowing brow in confusion up to you.)

TECHNICAL SUPPORT FOR STUDENTS

After (or while) focusing on gaining access to the right HIVE, instructors also have to line up some technical support for students. Like a napkin at an outdoor picnic, some might optimistically think they don't need it, but all will and you don't want to be caught without it.

Support can be anything from providing help with logins and passwords to making sure browsers are up to date and software is installed correctly. Support can be needed because the computer doesn't have the necessary capability, there are problems logging on, the right browser isn't installed, or an update for Flash or DirectX is missing. Some hard-to-diagnose problems can occur if a student is running a processor-intensive program in the background, like a 3-D golf game.

Support is especially tricky because professors are often less technically literate than their students. As with instructor manuals, the role of technical support can come from many sources. One solution is to set up or use a third-party support system, as is often provided by vendors. But if the simulation is free or heavily discounted, the support is inevitably lacking.

If the professor is indeed the point person, he or she must know how to access the software and be aware of the two or three most likely problems. Where possible, a teaching assistant who is technically literate and has more free time can take on this troubleshooting role. He or she can be directly connected to a support community, formal or informal. If a TA is the tech support, make sure his or her name is well distributed to all students.

Some organizations have computer technical support groups that can take over this burden as well. They just need to be briefed before they are called. They hate surprise calls. Really.

On top of the need to line up a troubleshooter, the reality of technical glitches makes it absolutely critical that students install or access any software at least twenty-four hours before they need to use it. For example, if students will be using an environment for the first time in the classroom, it may make sense to schedule an installation or logon event at the end of the class immediately before it.

CHUNKING CONTENT

Any long interactive content, such as a stand-alone sim on leadership or a group activity in *Second Life* to build a giant model of a cell, has to be integrated with the curriculum. Instructors have to decide how many days will be spent on the activity, and for those virtual classes that have them, how much of the simulation will be spent during "live" (synchronous) class time versus chat rooms versus office hours versus homework, and how the simulation itself will be punctuated by classrooms.

As a simple example, imagine a single-player asynchronous simulation, with no built-in synchronous pieces, that takes fifteen hours to engage. Imagine now that it is to be deployed in a classroom that meets for one 120-minute session once a week. This brings up quite a few possibilities and permutations. Should the entire simulation be played between two synchronous classes? Or should students engage half of the simulation, then attend a class, and then play the second half of the simulation? How should "live" synchronous events, if they are to be included, be allocated and best used?

Students in simulations go through cycles of frustration and resolution (as we discussed starting on page 40, and which we will talk a bit more about these later). In the "lows," students are most prone to quitting the sim, but they are also on the verge of coming to a resolution, which results in new mental muscles being formed (see the squiggly line on Figure 7.1).

The waves of highs and lows can be fairly predictable, especially on the third or fourth iteration of using a sim. Lows typically come around installing, accessing,

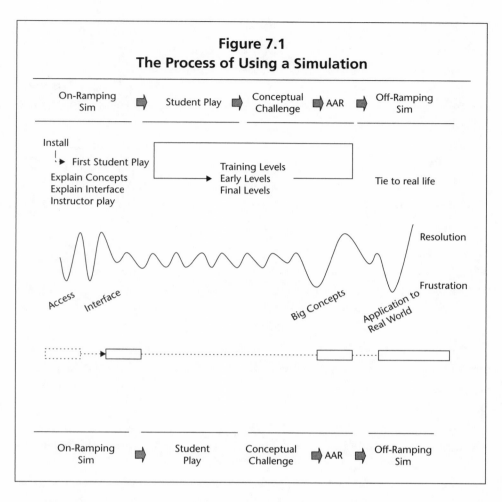

Figure 7.1
The Process of Using a Simulation

or teleporting to the sim for the first time, around using the interface, around every major new concept, and often when the student is challenged to create a strategy to apply the content to real life.

Thus, synchronous events such as classrooms (face to face or virtual, represented as the rectangles in Figure 7.1) should be used first to launch the simulation, then a little bit after each major frustration point as an After Action Review, and finally to tie the sim back to real life. In completely asynchronous environments, instructors may have to use office hours or proactively reach out to students via e-mail in anticipation of these lows.

Collaborative or team-based sims, in contrast to the single-player scenario, offer a further level of chunking requirements, often by the students in off-class (i.e., homework or lab) time. Suppose a sim on running a hospital is made up of ten turns, with each turn requiring team collaboration, and the entire sim has to be completed in two weeks. Instructors may assign one turn a day for five days a week. However, this requires a significant "live" commitment from the students (which is one reason the University of Phoenix minimizes use of this model and prefers the more self-paced branching models).

Some sims end with a big aha or gotcha (a lesson that if known about beforehand could subvert the learning), in contrast to sims aimed at practice. To prevent cheating or other bypassing of the learning goals, their content should be engaged in a proctored and synchronous environment.

Using Games at Points of Stress

There is another way, perhaps a better way, to deal with the moments of high frustration. Class games and activities, typically between five and twenty minutes long, are often a better option either right before or during moments of high frustration to both release stress and get to resolution more quickly.

Many class games are specifically aimed at reducing the frustration of learning an interface. For example, to teach students how to use the building authoring tools, they may be given the task of creating their own version of an existing object in *Second Life*. Or students may be asked to draw a face on the screen of a virtual classroom session to learn how to use the markup tools. Or to e-mail a screenshot as a postcard. To make the task more fun, students may be broken into teams and given time limits.

Later on, students may be given a brainstorming game to identify terms they have learned so far in a word jumble. Or to compete in a simplified version of the sim.

Printable Guides and Workbooks in Simulation Deployment: Friend or Foe?

Finally, the instructor has to think about support material. At the very least, a good downloadable tip sheet can save a bit of aggravation. But what about a workbook or guide? That's a good question.

Printed workbooks and guides are so, well, 1990s. They are packages of, gasp, paper (even if printed from PDF originals). They have the old-fashioned inputs like check boxes and blank places to write free-form text.

Their pages are bound together, forcing linear access. They cannot be graded electronically. If you find a mistake in a published guide, you can't correct it instantly.

In contrast, when one thinks of simulation deployments, one thinks of completely online experiences. Participants might get a CD-ROM, DVD-ROM, or ideally just a link. The experience should be futuristic. Any help is just-in-time and on the screen.

So why do I have the nagging feeling that workbooks and work guides will play an integral part in simulation deployments in the years to come? I guess because they have so many advantages. It is hard to break out of the simulation once you are in it. The very immersiveness of the simulation can almost trap players. Therefore, having a parallel content source, providing help, asking questions, guiding thoughts, and giving tips makes a huge amount of sense. In addition, printed guides are familiar. They are paper-based. They are comfortable. In the potential chaos of the simulation and other electronic environments, the paper can almost be reassuring.

Workbooks and guides provides a lasting artifact. Even after the link is lost and the simulation put away, the pages provide immediate reminder of the activities. And workbooks are easy and cheap to update, especially for a professor. Workbooks are often created in PowerPoint or Word. To change a term, a definition, even lesson plans, it can be much easier to do it in the paper world than in the electronic world. A single workbook can also tie together three or four disparate simulations.

The theorists will probably suggest that most if not all positive attributes of printed workbooks or guides, including those listed here, can ultimately be subsumed in the simulation itself, including support pages before and after any core gameplay. And I can't disagree. But my practical side has a sneaking suspicion that workbooks used in conjunction with simulations will be around for quite some time.

Perhaps the killer app in support of workbooks is that, increasingly, professors will access sims the way they access textbooks—as off-the-shelf finished products. The only way, or at least the best way, to customize the experience will be through other artifacts. In some cases professors may go through the basic play themselves. For example, they may take the entire class through the first level. Whether the guide is a one-page handout or a full tome, decide on your own level of need and desire. Then if you need one, build it.

Figure 7.2
A Page from a Workbook Supporting SimuLearn's vLeader

Using the Real-time Feedback

In the top right hand corner there is an EKG shaped feedback monitor. Use this feedback system to monitor the principles of power and tension.

Orange line – Tension of the character's present

Brown line – personal influence (referent power)

Green line – group's opinion of you (relational power)

Try Using Power

Power is an important component of getting things done. Collaborate to build informal power to help Will Dunn to get all of the right work accomplished.

☐ Select and Complete Practice Session Four (Gaining and Sharing Power)

Collaborate with Will to get both the COMBINE SALES and CONSOLIDATE IT ideas completed.

In what order did you complete the ideas?

_____

When did your personal influence go up (brown line)? Where were you clicking?

_____

When did Will's opinion of you go up (green lines)? Where were you clicking?

_____

When is the best time to introduce an idea you believe is important but is less popular with someone else?

_____

These exercises get more challenging. If you do not get the result you want, try it again and do something different. You may email a professional coach at coach@simulearn.net for assistance.

PILOTING

The final part of prep work is piloting. Highly interactive virtual environments need to be piloted. They need to be tested to hone the process of deployment. In fact, they need to be piloted twice. They need to be tested first to make sure all the technical bugs and processes are smoothed out. And then they need to be piloted conceptually with a class to make sure they do what we say they can do.

Technical Pilots

Let me be more specific. A technical and process pilot will happen regardless of what you do. The only question is, do you want to pilot with a real class, or a test group?

Technical pilots should, as close as possible, resemble the real-world environments in which the simulations will be deployed. It is not enough, for example, to test a deployment that will be international by testing it in different locations in the same building.

Different browsers should be used in the technical pilot if different browsers will be used by the students. If the simulation requires the use of a network, make sure that the different firewalls, including corporate if some students access from their workplaces, will accept the network stream.

Stress testing is also critical. If 30 or 50 or 1,000 students will be accessing the content simultaneously, those are the conditions that need to be tested. However, stress testing servers in one environment before testing them in a distributed environment allows faster troubleshooting.

Also in doing a pilot, especially if using Web-based content, beware of *caching*. Caching is the process by which a local computer temporarily stores content that it pulls from the Internet. The reason caching can be tricky is as follows. The first time content is accessed remotely, the videos play choppily. The technical person makes a few adjustments and thinks she has solved the problem. The remote test user plays the video a second time and it runs smooth as butter. Ostensibly, it seems as if the problem is solved. In fact, the only reason the performance has improved is that the video has been cached in the local computer. When a student loads it for the first time, he or she will still have the choppiness problems. It is often worth running a free tool such as CCleaner (www.ccleaner.com) that cleans out all cookies and cached content before any final technical test implementation.

Making Sure the Communication Infrastructure Works

The next vital activity on the checklist is to make sure the communication infrastructures are working. Technologies that have to be considered for any good collaborative experience include

- message board/forums and chat rooms,
- instant messaging,
- application sharing (make sure screen-sharing technology includes the mouse position, which is critical for live demonstrations),
- separate virtual rooms for teams to break off into,
- telephone conference call number,
- voice-over IP,
- calendaring tools, and even, where appropriate,
- multiplayer mediation.

Some environments have their own built-in communication infrastructure, such as their own version of instant messaging. But where possible, use instead the existing infrastructure students already use, including the tools included in the learning or class management system.

An in any kind of team-based project, a wise instructor will allow for both one-to-all communication and one-to-one communication. This is critical. Harvard Business School Publishing's Denis Saulnier explains why:

> If a team leader turns out to be overbearing, we will see individual team members chatting with each other about that behind the leader's back. That becomes an important dynamic in terms of how the simulation is played. Now whether or not to save those side conversations and make them available to the instructor has become a point of great interest. Currently we do not do that. Most of the faculty members believed that students had to feel as if that communication was truly private, even in a distributed environment. But others are trying to figure out some way of capturing that information, and we may just do it in an anonymous way, or perhaps aggregated way, at some point the future.

A Harvard Business School Publishing/Boston College distributed-learning pilot used both Web chat and speakerphone. Students very quickly learned to comfortably use both media. Typically, comments for the entire group were spoken and comments to individual team members were typed.

Conceptual Pilots

Although the technical pilot is critical, the pilot that more people will care about is the conceptual pilot. This piloting is the last step before a major rollout, with either a 10 percent or a 30-person sample of representative participant members (whichever is smaller), running the program exactly as you intend the full program to be but measuring the results at the end more rigorously.

The process of the conceptual pilot will match very closely, hopefully identically, the final rollout, as described in the next section on simulation deployments. Use that section to guide your conceptual pilot process. When HIVEs are short, such as ideas for new class games, they can also be tested in a pre-class session. If the students are asked to log in ten minutes before the class starts, they can be used as a test audience for a later class.

The results of a pilot can be used to make a "go/no go" decision if an organization is evaluating a sim or to practice and calibrate the sim before the full rollout (these are very different goals, and they do affect the feel of the conceptual pilot if not the steps). If the sim is being calibrated and significant changes are made, another pilot deployment is suggested before a major rollout.

As a quick note, when piloting a sim, it is critical not to say to the participants, "We are piloting this program. What do you think?" Instead, it should be positioned similarly to the major rollout, such as "This is the required program. Do your best."

CONCLUSION: THE NEED FOR FRONT LOADING

There are a lot of steps in preparing. It seems like a lot of work, and it is. But there are two comforting pieces of news: The first is that by preparing well, you will save yourself a lot of headaches later on. The second piece of good news is that once you have done this, in most cases you won't have to do it again for the same sim.

Like parenting, simulation deployment tends to be front loaded. This is a theme we will come back to in Chapter 9. Some instructors will even feel guilty later on when their students are working hard and they have nothing to do.

A Brief Example of a Simulation Deployment

Before we go into a formal process for using interactive environments, I would like to share an example. I like it not for its complexity but for its elegance and accessibility. It is a great example of "living off the land." It describes a stand-alone sim with a community tool, but it applies to any virtual environment.

PETER SHEA'S SIM FOR WRITING

St. Petersburg College's Peter Shea teaches both face-to-face and distant classes on writing. He noticed that beginning writers struggled with juggling two activities that traditionally happened simultaneously: generating ideas in writing and recognizing what rhetorical devices should be used and where. As a response he built a simple branching simulation and a rich community-based program around it. Here are the details.

The Setup

In this program, students first hear a lecture setting up the content and process. They also hear what Shea wants to accomplish with the simulation. "I also point out flaws of the simulation beforehand," Shea notes. "The students will if I don't."

Accessing the Sim

Then the students log onto the sim by following a link. Part of Shea's role is technical support. While he created the simulation in Adobe Flash, Shea also created an HTML version, in parallel, for students who were having trouble with Flash. But Shea subsequently found he could correct all the problems students had with Flash by asking them to go to the Adobe website and download the current version.

First, Self-Paced Student "Play"

The students are given the mission to write a letter to recommend a friend for a job that she really wants. In the sim, the students accomplish the "writing" by selecting a series of multiple-choice options. For example, students are first given three choices for potential introductions. Then they are given three more choices for the body of the letter.

The students do the simulation on their own. During the period the sim covers, Peter Shea is on call, as he says, 24/7. "The online student has very different expectations of office hours then the face-to-face student." So he tries to respond to all e-mail inquiries from his class within 24 hours.

The process of making choices around composition creates a very specific document. The simulation produces not only the text of the letter but also a short number that identifies the path each student takes.

Team Work

Shea's next step is to assign people who wrote the same documents to the same groups. The instructions had been something like, "Make sure you engage the simulation by Thursday." Then on Thursday evening, Shea asks everyone to begin the process of defending his or her decision. It is not acceptable to just say "I agree"; the argument has to be more substantial.

As is often the case, most of the value of (and the evaluation of the students in) this simulation is not the experience of the simulation per se but the interactions around the simulation with both peers and the instructor. The simulation just creates the context for better conversations. "Therefore" Shea adds, "it is key to very quickly link the simulation activity to a discussion board or list. This has to be done more deliberately than in the face-to-face environment where the conversations more spontaneously follow the simulation activity."

Coaching

Shea rigorously follows up with students who are not participating in the chat room. He tracks activity and sends e-mails asking why they have not gotten involved, with a reminder that they really need to get involved immediately.

"This is a momentum-based activity and I need to keep the momentum going," says Shea, who has been known to badger some student many times a day until he gets a response.

Shea has had to use both carrots and sticks. He might say to a student, "If you respond immediately I'll give you a certain number of points, and if you don't you will lose those points." In other cases, "I have shipped the student a Starbucks card for getting involved at the right time."

If students are having trouble articulating their decision, Shea might ask questions via e-mail, such as "What was going on in your head? Give me the movie of your mind."

Students' Graded Work

The groups end up with a defense of why they believe their choices created the best possible document for the situation. Although there is no one single right answer, there are shades of gray and a few wrong paths. Each group then posts its rationale in a common area.

Shea provides feedback to each group about their rationale. He can do this in writing, but increasingly he uses audio feedback via an MP3 file (perfect for students steeped in an on-demand culture). Finally, after the simulation activity when students have become comfortable with structuring documents, each student has to rerun the letter simulation and then write his or her own rationale for the new decisions made.

ONLINE VERSUS FACE TO FACE

Shea uses this content in both classroom-based and online environments. He has found that online students are very grateful for the interactivity, especially given how dull most of online content is: "I get feedback from students who were just so happy they have some type of content that is richer than uploaded online slides. What I've found is since the bar for online learning has been set so low, students have greatly appreciated every effort I have made to make the content more attractive. Students see this as being above and beyond what they get in other courses. When this kind of stuff becomes the norm, I suspect I'll receive less praise from students."

"Ultimately," he continues, "the opportunity for simulations is the feedback. The value that most professors in writing classes can provide is intelligent comments on the students' work. And as the volume of students we have to handle goes up, our ability to give that level of feedback has gone down. By using the simulation itself to provide a basic and broad level of feedback, we as instructors can focus on the highest-value and personalized comments."

STUDENTS AS REAL-TIME EVALUATORS OF SIMS?

I think this example provides a lot of lessons for many people using simulations. However, I would like to present one place where Shea and I, at least on the surface, disagree. I will also say that just because we disagree, I do not suspect he is in any way wrong. You should deliberately make your own choice.

Shea asks for ongoing feedback from his students. And he has found it very valuable to let students know that their voices are being heard. He lets students know that they can shape the course and therefore they take a more active role in the content, unlike traditional courses where students do not feel a level of engagement or ownership. Shea says, "I hope to show the students that the feedback they gave at the beginning of the class has already impacted the design of my learning objects that they encounter in the middle of the class."

This is in contrast to my own philosophy and experience. I have found that the best deployers of simulation are those who take a tough love approach around the content (students should still get help with any technology issues). They say literally, "Here is a simulation—you will not know what to do at times. You will be frustrated. You may think the simulation is broken. I don't want to hear any whining. Don't come to me when you are stuck. I can almost assure you that you will work through your frustrations yourself. And only by working through them yourself will you learn anything." It typically takes even a seasoned instructor about three semesters to develop the confidence to get to the point of this tough love philosophy of simulation use, to get to the point where they believe in that approach enough to present the attitude to the students. Put bluntly, I have found that either instructors develop this attitude and embrace frustration as the right path to resolution and enlightenment, or they remain apologetic, provide easy answers, and soon stop using the simulations altogether.

The Processes of Using a HIVE and the Role of Coaching

This chapter will go through the specifics of using a simulation with a class. It will start with the setup, the sim itself, and the After Action Reviews (also called debriefing). The process was first introduced in Chapter 7 (Figure 7.1).

THE SETUP

First, setting up a sim well is necessary for success. Instructors have to worry about both the technical setup and the instructional setup. In virtual environments deployment, get the access issues out of the way well before the real learning has to take place

Especially in a synchronous classroom situation, nothing gets in the way of a student learning from a simulation more than getting hung up on the technical issues. Most technical issues emerge when a student first engages a sim. They can take up significant time, typically requiring one-on-one help and leaving the rest of the class sitting around losing interest.

The technical issues should be completely resolved before the target class starts. This can be done in a number of ways:

- Students can be assigned to access the simulation and perform some simple test before they start class.

- There can be an optional event between normal classes dedicated to getting everyone accessing the simulation. This can be by appointment or at one scheduled time.

- Some professors dedicate a bit of time at the end of the class immediately before the simulation use to chaperon access or installation issues. Although this cuts into a bit of class time and can preclude students who have to rush off to their next class, it nonetheless provides a level of handholding and troubleshooting.

Regardless of how technical issues are resolved, it is expected that in all classroom deployments at least 10 percent of students will have technical difficulties accessing a new simulation, and it will take one technical person around fifteen minutes of dedicated time to solve the problem.

Softly Bringing People into *Second Life*

Inviting people, including students and even guest speakers, into *Second Life* can be more complicated than accessing a stand-alone sim. In a perfect world, there is no better way to transition someone into *Second Life* than a one-on-one guide. Have someone there when the person first arrives.

For a guest speaker, as an example, this should typically be a week before participation is needed. They need to get comfortable walking around, using voice over IP (VoIP), and using chat. It is also useful to make sure that any subject-matter expert has a physical headset. Talking someone through their introduction to *Second Life* is much more efficient than hyping it to them. "I can't tell you the number of people to whom I say, we're going to be online on Monday and make sure you have headphones. Then come Monday they show up and they don't have headphones," says Robert Bloomfield, professor at Cornell's Graduate School of Management. "So I ask the speaker about this and they say 'Don't worry, my computer has a microphone' which, of course, produces a terrible sound." You need a headset to have the sound quality work in *Second Life*.

Don't Adjust the Settings!

Some of the biggest complaints about the *Second Life* experience come when students adjust their setting. As a rule, strongly suggest that students only minimally adjust the recommended screen and audio settings.

The Intellectual Setup

Setting up a simple class game is pretty easy. Present the students with simple, verb-centric instructions like these:

- *Write* three words on screen.

- *Circle* other people's words that best describe the situation.

This setup gets a bit harder with more complicated experiences. Students often enough hear about the simulation before they enter the first class. They tend to be both excited and apprehensive about it. This can cause a problem, as the students will want to rush through any pre-work. This student desire can simply be acknowledged, or students can be given a small sample level (sometimes called *training level* or *simple first level*) showing a basic interface with a basic goal to satiate this need.

There are many competing ways to introduce the concepts of simulations to a class. Instructors almost always present the basic framework and timelines of the simulation: how long it will take, how it will be graded, assignments to teams, and how to access the simulation.

Instructors then have to decide how much of the sim experience they want to explain up front. In some cases, such as the classic "beer game," a supply chain management simulation (perhaps best described in Senge 1990), the lessons learned from the simulation are a surprise and are much more effective when discovered organically. In other cases, such as the example of the baseball batting cage, there are no big ahas or gotchas to ruin, and the goal is practice and refinement.

It is harder to figure out how much to explain when the simulation is somewhere in the middle. If the simulation uses a complex system, for example, should the instructor detail that system or not? There is no right answer. As a broad rule, adult learners typically like to have the theory presented before they engage the system in a simulation. Younger students tend to like to play around first in the simulation and only then be presented with "the answer."

Set the Tone

Throughout the process, set the tone carefully and find the student value in every stage. Brock Dubbels (whom you met in Chapter 2) says, "When I start using words like *game* and *play,* the impact is very different" from the traditional school talk. He did a little experiment with some engineering students. In one class he said, "I think we are going to have a lot of fun today. The first thing I what you to do is open your kit up and play around with it." In the other class he said, "We are really under deadline today. There is a lot of work to do. You need to be introduced to your tools and then hear the outcomes we need to achieve." Brock found that the two groups approached the situation very differently. The challenge is that many professors take what they do so seriously, and they may inadvertently kill the potential fun of the simulation.

ON RAMP: FROM REAL LIFE TO SIMULATION

With those basics out of the way, the instructor is now able to launch from the distributed classroom setting (such as WebEx, Elluminate, or *Second Life*) into the simulation (such as the ones from Forio/Harvard Business School Publishing or in *Second Life*). At this point, instructors also start the shift from lecturer to true coach. The first priority is to smoothly "on ramp" the student from the real world to the simulation (Figure 9.1).

The best simulation coaches start off by connecting the sim to the real world. Dan Smith, the founder and president of Capsim, gives the following speech as an introduction to a business simulation, typically to business students:

> I have been running companies for over 30 years. And in my business career, I have made mistakes. So let me tell you what the worst day is going to be in your business life. It is going to be the day that you have to call someone into your office and you will say to them, "You are fired." When they ask you why, you are going to say, "You are fired because I made a mistake. I screwed up and I have to let some people go. I know this is going to affect your career. It is going to impact your family life. And I am genuinely sorry. But you are fired because I screwed up." My goal is to have you face that situation in a business simulation so that you don't have to face it in real life.

This connects the students to some kind of reality to which they can personally relate. A variation is to engage the students' own experiences. For example, imagine a simulation where the participants have to negotiate peace between two warring factions. There are a number of ways for the coach to tap into the students' experiences:

- Ask for personal stories or opinion: "Have you ever been in a fight with someone and you just got stuck in a cycle of violence?"

- Ask the class to define the value of the activity: "Across history, what was the most wasteful war, in terms of resources spent and the lack of real gains accomplished?"
- Ask for a definition: "How would you define a successful peace negotiation? What would the outcome look like?"
- Set up a mock debate: "I want half the class to argue that appeasement is a good strategy, and the other half to argue that going to war is a good strategy."
- Have students write down a lingering problem or question. "With whom right now, in your personal life, are you in a fight? You don't have to share it with the class, but you do have to pick a real example."
- Or the coach could ask, "What concept in the literature are you having the most trouble understanding?"

It is critical to draw everyone in. Ideally, the students will feel some ownership. Anyone who sits out during this part probably will not be engaged later in the process.

TEACHING THE INTERFACE

Interfaces are one of the biggest paradoxes in simulations. The more intuitive the interface is to use in the final level, the less the student will probably learn from the simulation.

Why? One of the big ahas of the next generation of content designers is that the interface should be a significant piece of the content, not just a conduit to the content. The interface should line up to the real-life activity at some level, high or low, to enable transferability of content. If students already understand all their potential actions before they begin the sim, then perhaps the sim interface should be more ambitious.

Consequently, the interface should be taught as valuable content, not just apologized for as being a potentially clunky access point. The same approach to teaching the invisible and underlying system should be used for teaching the interface. Instructors will want to show a screenshot. They may want to take the class through a few actions. They will want to draw analogies to people's own lives.

FIRST PUBLIC SIMULATION PLAY

Whether or not students have played a first level on their own, a good coach will often orchestrate and narrate a synchronous group simulation play. This is a short example or single turn of the sim, ideally with limited choices, a clear goal, and clear feedback. The whole level should take about five minutes.

After the coach sets up the situation, he or she might use one of at least four variations:

- *The coach can use the controls, talking through the actions.* Here, the coach takes over and plays through the level, talking aloud about various decisions. This is the fastest approach, and the easiest, but the least interactive.

- *The coach can use the controls, asking the group what to do.* This focuses the group on the strategic aspects of the simulation, although it can gloss over interface issues.

- *An individual student can be chosen to take the controls and play through the level.* This demonstrates a "real" person using the interface, making common mistakes and common discoveries. It builds community and even sympathy. It also focuses the group on the interface issues as well as the strategic ones.

- *An individual can be chosen to take the controls, but told by the group what to do.* This has all the advantages of the other approaches, but it can also take the longest, sometimes building impatience in the group.

Perfect Play, Good Enough, or Intentional Failure?

In this first option above for the initial public play, it is up to the coach whether the goal is a perfect play, good enough, or outright failure.

A perfect play shows the class that perfection is possible (and that the coach knows how to do it perfectly). This can be useful if the first level is a bit challenging, especially if students have already accessed the level and have been frustrated with it. The students have gained confidence, but now they are likely to skip to the still harder second level, sometimes not fully prepared or not having learned the critical lessons of the first level.

Deliberately failing creates a different dynamic (I don't mean to brag, but I am really good at deliberately failing.) It can create in the students the unresolved tension and desire to "solve the puzzle." Students may look less to the coach for answers and more toward each other. Still, if the first level is hard, failure in the first public play may convince some that it is too hard, creating intellectual dropout. If the coach fails, he or she has to point out some of the bad decisions along the way. Thus the coach may note, "I know that X, but I don't care. I am going to do Y." If a coach publicly fails, students have to know exactly where and why. (There are times, especially in a real-time simulation, when the coach may try to win in front of the class but actually fails. In a real-time, dynamic simulation, this is easier than you might think.)

The middle ground, and perhaps the sweet spot, is ending up with a good-enough play. The play is successful but not the best possible. If there is a score, it is in the 85 percent range. If there is a balanced scorecard methodology (in our peace simulator, for example), one factor may outstrip others ("volume of violence" may go down, an indicator of success, but "establishment of local government" may also remain down, an indicator of failure). This good-enough-play method is also effective if some type of label can be put on the middle strategy ("I suppose appeasement did not completely work here").

PUTTING TOGETHER GROUPS FOR MULTIPLAYER OR TEAM-BASED SIMS

Now students are ready to try their own hand, usually at one specific level. Students often need to be organized into teams or buddy groups. The groups can be self-organized by students, randomly organized, or engineered.

For student-organized teams, the instructor may put a sign-up sheet on the screen and give students a chance to write in their names. Students may have bid on each other in past simulation deployments as a method for grading.

Instructors who engineer groups use criteria including interpersonal compatibility, balancing of strengths, and most importantly what time off-class the students have available in a given week, including time zones and other schedule obligations. Or teams may be chosen either to maintain or break up previous loyalties (all French students or all Australian students). And some teams are just picked randomly.

Grouping (often just as important in single-player as in multiplayer sims) can include the following configurations.

Matching People with Buddies

Buddies are a group of two or three participants who agree to help each other out during the course of an educational experience.

The buddy relationship can be short term: buddies might share a screen or meeting room and provide feedback and comments. In some cases, the relationship might just be to help each other figure out basic inputs and actions.

The buddy relationship can also continue for weeks or even months: buddies can virtually follow up with each other to make sure they are completing assignments and applying the material and to act as a constant muse. They can read and comment on each others' blog entries.

The buddy relationship can also be informal or formal. The more important the material learned, especially when big skills are being covered, the more important the role and responsibility of buddies.

Setting Up Teams

Teams are groups of people who have tied their relative success to each other. People in teams typically play different roles—such as leaders and followers—and perform different technical tasks.

"When people are organized into teams," notes Dan Smith, founder and president of Capsim, a vendor of leading virtual business simulations, "they increase their engagement, their bandwidth. That's why team sports are so memorable."

The coach may group students into teams and perhaps even assign roles within the team. Most simulation teams ideally are about five people.

While the role of teams is critical and obvious in extensively team-based simulations, teams also have a very important role in single-player sims. In a single-player sim, teams can have collective responsibilities to achieve certain thresholds, either individually or collectively, and therefore take responsibility for each other's performance.

The coach may also help the group come up with (or assign the group to figure out) a regular time to meet "virtually but same time" (synchronously) during the course of the simulation deployment. A one-hour conference call once a week can mean the difference between success and failure in the simulation deployment.

Competitors

Not the be-all zero-sum or anything, but often when there is one team, there are other teams. And often these teams are competing with one another. And competition, a game element, triggers motivation. In some sims, competition also forces a team to adapt to strategies based on the changing conditions put forth by another team.

Here are two caveats about competition around sim play. The first is that in a competitive environment, students typically worry less about learning the content and more about reverse engineering the simulation and trying to optimize the score. The second is that ground rules need to be established to keep friendly competition from becoming unfriendly.

COACHING DURING THE STUDENT USE

Like a parent, after you have prepared your students as much as possible, you must thrust them into the unforgiving simulated world. Your own role diminishes considerably as your students take up a lot of the responsibility for their own results. There are, however, a few things to look out for as you scan the activity.

The Right Amount of Hand-Holding

One interesting skill to hone is how much hand-holding to offer. Typically, in their first one or two deployments of the simulation, professors act like a parent of a first child. They offers a tremendous amount of hand-holding for every step of the way. They want to IM everyone. They visit each group virtually.

And then, at least with good simulations, by the time instructors teach a simulation the third or fourth time, they are more like the parent of a third child. They are much more willing to say, "Here's a simulation. You won't always know what to do. That's part of the learning and welcome to life. Work through all the problems yourself." Curiously enough, most students don't want suggestions initially—they want to forge their own path. Only when they make a massive mistake are they receptive to advice.

Ongoing Roles: Tracking and Questioning

One role the instructor needs to continue, however, is tracking to make sure that all students are engaged and none are forced into "cram" situations, when simulations work remarkably poorly.

Another ongoing role for a coach (and some would say the only real role) is to ask questions. These questions can be aimed at individual students or, better, to the group as a whole. Some good questions ask about long-term issues, such as "What is the break-even point for the product you are currently developing?" Other good questions follow the driving instructor model: "Why did you just do that?"

If a student does something either right or wrong, and the instructor notices it either through screen sharing or more likely from looking at a dashboard of some type, the instructor can ask, "What did you hope would happen? What is your thinking right now?" These moments of forced reflection can break the student out of a mindless clicking mentality that seizes most simulation players at some point. Such questions are ideally asked "live" through messaging tools or less well through synchronous tools such as e-mail or chat rooms.

A variation of this is to role-play, often through e-mails, a stakeholder, such as a customer, a constituent, or a board member. Then specific questions can be asked from a specific point of view that has a high emotional stake. "Why are you supporting the opposing party? Don't you know they are corrupt? I hate you," an e-mail or MP3 voice message from a citizen might say.

Instructors can get at the behavior of the simulation by asking, "Why do you think the simulation did that?" Or "What are the important variables being tracked here?" Such questions are especially powerful when students are having differing experiences from each other and are becoming confused and frustrated.

Extra Bonus Challenges for the Top 20 Percent

Good coaches may also notice that some students are excelling more rapidly than the rest of the class. They might decide to make things more challenging for those students. For example, they might say, "Play the sim again, but don't use any of resource X." Or "Try to accomplish the same goal you just accomplished but in half the time."

Highlight Mistakes for the Amusement and Education of the Group

Highlighting the mistakes of one group for the entire class has multiple benefits. First, it is fun for almost everyone. Second, it is educational. People do learn from others' mistakes. Third, it increases the sense of tension and risk, which increases the emotional stakes of the experience and therefore increases learning. The only caveat is to give fair warning and tell students before the simulation starts that you might do this. "We are evil. We like to embarrass people," jokes Dan Smith.

Ongoing Player Comparison

When multiple students or teams are engaging either competitively or with the same experience, it is useful to share some aspect of each other's progress or lack thereof. This can be the sharing of key metrics each turn. It can be a high score list. It can even be "headlines" such as "Team A scores a major victory" or "Team B faces major fine for ethics violations."

Managing the Bottom 20 Percent

There is almost inevitably a group of students, typically about 20 percent, who do not buy into the learning experience and mentally drop out. When asked a reasonable question, they don't know what is going on.

In a classroom, this group can sit (sometimes virtually) in the back, and most instructors quietly ignore them. They doodle or write e-mails.

In an environment with simulations that is based on constant "doing," this group can become vocal opponents, criticizing the validity of the simulation. In the worst case, they may even lead a revolt. Often, some of these students are frustrated leaders. So putting them in leadership positions can help resolve the problem. Other times, they might just need more coaching. The first option is to pair them up with a high-performing team. If that doesn't work, they should be given easier goals, and they should be met with offline for more one-on-one interaction.

AFTER ACTION REVIEWS

Once the students are done with a level, it is time for an After Action Review (AAR in Figure 7.1).

After Action Reviews (also called *debriefings*) are a pedagogical technique of using focused sessions, typically after the core gameplay implementation, so students will better understand what happened and what should have happened. This can include strategic implications.

An AAR is essential when a simulation produced high amounts of frustration, and even more necessary when the simulation ended with some students still quite frustrated. The coach has to present why things got so frustrating and how it ties back to the real world.

AARs in a sim usually require a combination of human and computer intervention. But one or the other can do in a pinch.

Further, ideally, participants give the first analysis of their own performance, before the coach does. One of the changes as simulations move online, however, is that both the student/team self-evaluation and the coach's evaluation are often

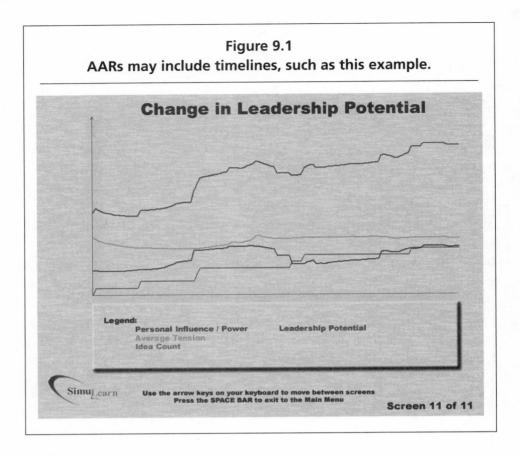

Figure 9.1
AARs may include timelines, such as this example.

done asynchronously, and recorded MP3s are becoming the communication vehicle of choice. These "podcasts for one" can capture the humanity of a live conversation with the convenience of self-paced communication.

AARs risk either being too positive or too negative. They are more useful when they are both "thumbs up, thumbs down," a phrase from parts of the military meaning "Here is one positive thing and here is one thing to change."

Feedback in AARs can include the following:

• raw material, such as recorded plays and timelines,

• analysis (what happened and why at a thematic level),

• coaching (how to get better results next time, and perhaps how to transfer to real-life situations from the perspective of an expert or peers),

- evaluation for certification (the player's readiness to handle real situations), and even

- game elements like a high score or rewards and recognition, which can spur competition and replay/redo.

For practice-based sims, AARs should be used often enough to force users to think about their performance and then have the opportunity to try again.

Denis Saulnier of Harvard Business School Publishing gives an example from their Everest multiplayer simulation: "Teaching soft skills involves more room for interpretation, and therefore the After Action Reviews are more critical. The experience is more of a black box for the users than more mechanical sims, because of the points system that we use to evaluate each person's performance on the team." He continues, "Sometimes a player is forced to be rescued, and he or she might not even know why. In the debriefing, the professor can see what happened and explain."

Finally, use the manual, if one is available, for probing questions. As a general rule, the less the instructor talks and the more the students talk, the more successful the AAR is.

OFF RAMP: FROM SIMULATION BACK TO REAL LIFE

The instructor's final activity in the context of the simulation is to wrap up the entire experience by tying it to real life. At the beginning of the simulation launch, the instructor tries to go from real life to simulation. Now he or she has to do the opposite: go from simulation to real life. There are a number of ways to do this:

- Ask the students what they have learned and what they see and do differently as a result: "Can I see a show of hands how many people have learned about X?"

- Highlight some great plays (or at least great results) and shared humor: "Remember when team X accomplished this? I bet no one thought that was even possible."

- Recall the content from the on-ramping session, and ask if any of the personal challenges brought up then can now be resolved: "Go back to your notes. Look at what you wrote down before we started the sim. That thing that was a big challenge, that concept that was hard to get, is it any more clear now?"

- Highlight the key lessons learned: "We have learned X, Y, and Z."
- Get students focused on next steps, if any, including an action plan.
- Let the students know how and when they can reaccess the sim and what help is available for them.

INTO THE BREACH

Many times, successfully using simulations means putting trust in things outside the coach's micromanagement. Nothing is harder for an instructor than to exchange the control of a lecture for the experience of a simulation. Likewise, to even ask a group of students, "What did you learn?" is emotionally harrowing. Any instructor worries about the devastating response of "Nothing." But with experience we learn to love the unknown.

Creating Evaluation Strategies

Instructors have to evaluate *students' performance*. But we, intrepid souls that we are, also have to do more. In these still early days of highly interactive virtual environments, we have to demonstrate (which requires measuring) the effectiveness of the *approach* so that we can perpetuate and grow our programs despite critics and get others to buy in to the approach. Finally, we have to *calibrate* any sim, which also requires assessment and evaluation strategies. Our successful advocacy of HIVEs requires not that we defend them blindly, but that we evolve them intelligently.

This chapter will discuss how and why and give examples of surveys and results. Before we get started, one might ask, why not do things the old easy-to-compare-to-traditional-methods way? Why not just use a standardized test? And should a simulation deployment be expected to beat a standard course assessment to prove that simulations work better?

WHY NOT MEASURE EXPERIENCE WITH A MULTIPLE-CHOICE TEST?

Let's start with that basic question. Why not just measure the newly acquired student knowledge through multiple choice questions, preferably using existing tests? After all, this objective methodology should settle the matter once and for all if simulations work better. In other words, as some of us have heard from numerous sources including deans, department heads, colleagues, and even our parents, "Why can't you just be normal?"

Measuring simulation learning through a multiple-choice post-test is almost futile. Designing pre- and post-tests for simulations can be an almost existential experience. What is it that the student has actually learned?

It is useful to think back to the example of driving a car (a learning-to-do activity rather than learning to know). First, driving a car is a perfect shared example of a complex skill. The actions of driving a car are well understood, and they are both discrete and analog, including turning the steering wheel the precise right amount and using the turn signal. The goal of driving a car is also very clear, such as getting to the right destination with no accidents and enough gas for the next trip. But the systems that connect actions and goals are incredibly (and appropriately) complex. They include everything from the timing of when to turn into a busy intersection (which involves predicting where every vehicle will be five to fifteen seconds in the future) to the strategies of planning the route for a long trip (including cultural knowledge of traffic congestion and construction) to the ethical and pragmatic decisions about speeding. (Given all of advantages of driving as an analogy, let's try to look past the two obvious problems. The first is that, except for those who are teaching a teenage daughter or son, exactly how much is involved is often lost because we do it so well. Second, driving is so, well, vocational If we had a better shared understanding, I would rather use a skill such as leadership, innovation, stewardship, even writing.)

Consequently, most multiple-choice tests about driving (such as in a driver's test) are about defining terms and articulating the rules of the road. Few paper tests, appropriately enough, aspire to measure how well a driver actually drives. That's why states use real, physical driving tests. Likewise, many excellent drivers would fail the written part of most driving tests.

So how do we, as users of interactive environments, create tests to measure timing, balance, and judgment? How do we get around the issue that, on paper, most of the questions just seem to be common sense?

To go back to the driving example, the cause of every single accident that ever has happened would not be among the options selected on a quiz. No one would choose (a) eat and put on makeup while driving, (b) text message friend instead of keeping eyes on road, or (c) tailgate driver in front of me so that if he stopped suddenly I would hit him. Yet the right sim could lower the number of accidents caused by these things.

I wish had a definitive answer, but I don't. The challenge of dismantling a system that is biased toward linear content is not going to be easy. Critical, yes. Easy, no.

We do have a lot of very good options. There are different approaches in creating an appropriate simulation evaluation strategy. Of course they should be around the core learning goals and program goals. But, pragmatically, they tend to be heavily influenced by the sometimes conflicting primary variables of *effectiveness, cost* (including political cost), *evaluation of program versus evaluation of student,* and *political and program expediency.*

Some of these approaches are unusual for a traditional class but are right at home for more intensive programs such as executive education and for instructors that need to build a real case. I am including a complete list to both challenge and inspire us. We ultimately need to learn how to measure "learning to do" as much as "learning to know."

ASSESSMENT STRATEGIES
Post-test Only or Also Pre-test?

Do you evaluate what the students started off knowing or just what they know after the end of the program? Any kind of certification program (whether in programming or awareness about sexual harassment) cares about only what the student knows at the end of the program. But any sim program manager also wants to know what the magnitude of the shift is. Some programs, as with the certification, get everybody past a threshold. Other programs help every student the same amount relative to their starting knowledge. So experts end up as advanced experts, and beginners end up as advanced beginners. Still other programs help experts more than beginners, or the other way around. Knowing the starting point of each student provides a much better understanding of the program's impact.

Control Group or Just Students?

Do you evaluate a group of people who did not go through the program as well as the students who went through the program? Any scientific validation requires a control group, but that often takes a lot of will on the part of the program manager.

"Students Only" or People Around Students?

Do you just use the students' own knowledge or insights, or do you tap the knowledge and insights of the people around the student (so-called 360s)? Students themselves tend to overvalue new knowledge and undervalue new actions, but for the communities around the students it is exactly the opposite.

Evaluate Right after the Program or Weeks or Months Out?

Do you administer any post-program evaluation the moment the program is over? Doing so will overemphasize the fast-decaying new knowledge acquired, while making impossible the evaluation of new behavior (unless the program has taken place over weeks, when new behavior might have already shown up). The more time after the program (one week, five weeks, five months), the greater the value of any recorded impact but the harder it is to get results (the compliance rate goes down), the harder it is to use those results to shape the program itself, and the more other variables get in the way. The greater the group involved in evaluating the student (the 360s), the more time is needed (if someone only meets with the student twice a month, it takes longer for them to see real changes).

Standardized Multiple Choice or Short Answers?

Do you ask everyone the same multiple-choice questions? This makes it easy to compare results. Or do you allow short answers? This adds more personality and allows for answers outside the standardized ones. It gathers anecdotes of success, which are great if (shudder) subjective.

Indicators or Direct Measurement?

Do you look at some sort of external objective measure? Success of student in subsequent classes? Success of student in workplace (if they are a part-time student or if they transition right from your class to the workplace)? Retention of student? Can this information be gathered through objective means?

Automated Questionnaire or Interview?

Do you create an online test and questionnaire? Or do you have real people involved? The first is cheaper but has a lower compliance rate. The second is much more expensive but more nuanced.

"Test" versus Reflection, Knowledge versus Behavior?

Do you ask questions like "What is the formal definition of _____?" Are you interested in making the students prove that they have learned something? Students who go through simulation experiences do understand the concepts very well, but simpler programs may get the same result. Instead of asking definitions, a richer approach is to present mini-situations that give the students the ability to decide what to do.

Are you asking questions like "How good are you at _____" and "How often in the last two weeks have you found yourself _____?" Do you want students to look at their own experience and draw conclusions? Unfortunately (and this is a true story) this subjective reflection in a pre-and-post situation can backfire. I have had students think they were a 4 out of 5 in leadership skills in the pre-test. Then they went through the program, learned a lot, and realized how much more they had to learn. Then in the post-test they claimed they were a 3 out of 5. During the program, they seemingly lost a point of leadership skills! (One option around that is to have students reevaluate their pre-program opinions in a post-test. Rather than just asking "How good a leader are you?" in both the pre- and post-tests, I also like to ask in the post-test "How good a leader were you before the program?" This can be compared to the respondents' original answer and shows an interesting delta.)

Student Opinion of the Class?

Through years of schooling, we are very aware when we learn new facts. We are less aware when we increase our abilities. It is quite possible for students to go through a program and not "learn" anything new but, as the result of the sim, to be much more effective because they now actively apply what they know. In their own review, such students might say, "This was all pretty basic," but their colleagues see a new person.

In the corporate world and any fluid hierarchical system, as I have said before, only one metric really matters: that the person responsible for the program gets promoted. Any other metric, be it smile sheets or increased organizational productivity or stock price, is only ammunition. Said another way, most evaluation is marketing for future programs.

ASSESSMENT TECHNIQUES FOR GRADING STUDENT PERFORMANCE

In most cases, professors need to grade the performance of a student in a simulation for the experience to be considered official. Although this grading is probably just as arbitrary as grading a paper, at least grading a paper has the benefit of history and precedent on its side.

Here are some assessment techniques for HIVEs.

Write a Paper about the Experience

In some cases, students can write a paper about their experience in a simulation. This is the most comfortable for most professors. The paper could be about why the player did what he or she did—justifying his or her actions. Students can also pull in traditional references to other literature, further making a comfortable fit into traditional academic environment. Likewise, students can write a competitive analysis of the sim situation for a business class or the history of an event for a political science class.

Keep a Journal during the Experience

A variation on a paper is to have the students keep a journal while they're playing the simulation, and the journal itself can be graded. The journal can discuss the experiences in the simulation, including frustrations met and resolutions delivered. Ideally, the students may also discuss their experiences in the real world as seen through the lens of the simulation. For example, if the simulation is on leadership, students may compare the experiences in the simulation with a real-life leadership experience, such as on a lacrosse team.

Create a Multimedia Production

Students can produce rich multimedia productions of their experiences and lessons learned. They can combine several media, including static screenshots, in-world video clips (perhaps gathered by using Fraps), real-world video and photographs, voiceover, text on screen, and even music. The production could be assembled with something as complicated as video editing software or as simple as PowerPoint. One could look to machinima, a genre of art where footage from modded computer games is edited together as a film, for inspiration.

These productions meet the needs of helping students learn to do, learn to be, and learn to know. They can be graded for intellectual integrity and aesthetic value. They can also be posted for other students to see.

Clearly, this is a new genre of homework. Critics (especially those who forget how bad most student homework assignments really are) will be critical about how superficial these artifacts may seem. And it will take some time for this new genre to find its legs. But if we truly believe in freeing up students, not just molding them, I think we will all be amazed at the kinds of intellectual properties that are created.

Peer Assessment

Professors can also use peers to assess one another. Here is an example of how one professor has used peer assessments.

PEER ASSESSMENTS OF INDIVIDUAL CONTRIBUTIONS TO TEAM PROJECT (WEIGHT TO BE APPLIED TO TEAM PROJECT GRADES):

Here is a description of a method from one professer: "Motivating individuals to contribute to a team effort requires values, norms, and systems that promote accountability. I can do little to directly affect the values and norms that individuals in your team adopt, but I can implement a reward system that holds individuals accountable for their contributions to your project. Each team member will be required to allocate points to represent the relative contributions teammates made to the project. The average of each person's ratings will be converted into a weight that will subsequently be applied to a team's project grade. An example should clarify this somewhat complex process

Let's say Team A has five members. Sue must rate each of the other four members of her team. She will be given 400 total points (100 per teammate) to allocate. If she believes each member contributed equally, she could simply assign 100 points to each person. In this case, each team member would receive 100 percent of the team's project grade (let's say 90 out of 100 points). However, if she believed two members worked much harder than the other two she could give the hard workers 110 points each and the slackers 80 points each. This would mean that the hard workers would earn 110% of the 90 points earned by the team project. This equals 99 points out of a possible 100. The slackers would only earn 72 points (80 percent of 90 points.)"

Time Spent in Simulation

Although measuring the amount of time spent with the simulation is unsatisfying intellectually, it may have the benefit of correlating to the highest future success. A variation of this approach is to set up markers throughout an island that record (and save to a Web page) whenever each student touches it. It turns out that the more students "play with their food before eating it," the more they learn.

Modify the Environment

Students can be asked to in some way improve the simulation, change the simulation, or make a new level for the simulation. In *Second Life,* for example, a team of students with basic software development skills (including identifying requirements, turning requirements into designs, managing intellectual resources, working with graphics packages, creating or editing light programs in *Second Life*'s object-oriented language, LSL) could build a working virtual lab.

Funny enough, this activity politically satisfies a lot of simulation critics in school systems. Professors can do a further rim shot by having students write up design documents to explain their simulation design. Boo-yah!

Most people, including many simulation experts, would say that making a simulation is a very powerful way of learning via the simulation experience. This process forces students to learn and research nonlinear content, as well as apply a first person perspective to content. Here again I disagree with many of my smarter and better-looking colleagues as being the highest goal of simulation technology. If you were coaching an Olympic athlete, you would not ask her to design the track, and you would not ask a pilot to design a flight simulator as part of his training (of course you want feedback for subsequent iterations of the simulation). Once you ask someone to be in design mode, you are forgoing the pure learning-to-do experience. The process of creating a simulation is very intellectual—a variety of learning to know. Still, given the biases of many schools toward learning to know and the production of media as work, this approach will for the foreseeable future be politically expedient.

Play the Simulation Well/Complete the Simulation

In some cases, how well a player does in a simulation could correlate directly with the grade. So in the simplest example, if the player got a 95 percent score in the simulation, he or she would get an A for the assignment. A variation is, depending on how the program is structured, if the student finishes the simulation, he or she would get an A. Although this raises many fidelity issues, perhaps these issues should be raised regardless. And certainly if I were doing a certification-based program, this would be the approach I would use.

This form of evaluation requires the simulation in some way to be online and able to reliably transmit the data to the professor. Some simulations go even further and provide very detailed information about student play.

Use Different Approaches

I think as we mature in this area the biggest challenge for any student and the behavior deserving of the greatest reward, especially in a liberal arts or business environment will be how well the student applies very different approaches for the same situation. And then (and only then), how well they identify a right approach for the situation, and then how well they execute it. I admit however this is still a ways off.

CONCLUSION

Two interesting trends face college instructors today. One is distributed classrooms, and the other is educational simulations. Both are high tech, and both require innovation. And both have the potential to re-create higher education. Typically, distributed classrooms are being pushed upon the instructors by the deans and department heads, while educational simulations are being driven by the instructors themselves. This difference, from a deployment perspective, changes everything.

Professors who are using distributed classes are getting a lot of hand-holding and support. Some schools set up mentoring programs. Department heads bend over backwards to set up flexible, virtual office structures. Help desks for students and instructors are available. And as part of the new deal, professors are given more freedom in areas such as assessment. In fact, professors of distributed classrooms are pioneering new assessment methodologies, in part due to the fact that all tests are open book, such as community collaboration and peer reviewing, team participation, and amount of new insight brought to a problem.

Simulation deployments, in contrast, are facing almost the opposite situation. Professors using simulations are viewed with suspicion, especially if the sims involve 3-D graphics and have other game attributes. Even their colleagues suspect that the instructors using sims have never grown up and just want an excuse to play games all day, or that they are dumbing down content for the sake of remedial students. And as for any technical support—fugettaboutit!

As a result, assessment programs have evolved in the exact opposite direction of those used in distributed classes. Any sim assessment has to make the case that simulations are better than traditional content. The tests have to be absolutely traditional, the more objective and standardized the better, to prevent any funny business. The tests that students take are as much to evaluate the sim methodology as the students' absorption of content.

The future of assessment of behaviors in virtual environments, Randy Hinrichs told me, is "real-time" and "long time." Every action of a student, from picking up an object to mixing chemicals to sitting in a chair to talking with teammates to participating in class to building a room is recordable. A student's navigation pattern can be tracked, both around a class and around a simulation. This will create new assessment methodologies truly around what a student does as well as what a student knows.

PART THREE

Other Considerations

Selling Interactive Environments Internally

Getting Buy In from Administrators, Department Heads, Colleagues, Parents, and Even Students

This chapter will describe best practices in building support for interactive environments and setting the appropriate expectations for various stakeholders. It will also put the concept of fun in the context of the content and address the issues of funding.

Instructors have acknowledged a lot of political concerns with using interactive environments, especially ones that are three dimensional, have a lot of quickly moving objects, and look a lot like computer games. John Kirriemuir (2005), a researcher in the use of computer and video games for learning and teaching, put together a list of concerns about adopting simulations:

1. Potential reaction from fellow instructors and governors.

2. Potentially adverse reaction from parents.

3. Lack of examples of real educational situations where games had been used successfully.

4. Possibly losing lesson control, and focus, to students who are far more familiar with the game.

5. Commercial games not being validated by education-oriented standards bodies.

6. Campus computers being insufficiently powerful to run contemporary computer games.

7. Faculty have to learn about games, and learn a game very well, in their own time.

8. The time consideration, with classroom timetables being "salami-sliced."

BUILDING SUPPORT FOR HIVEs

Today, adopting highly interactive environments requires some sales work. Here are some strategies for selling them to your department. And as a quick aside, some of the strategies are contradictory, so put together a plan that works for you.

1. Address Learning Goals

Almost every course has learning goals that have proven tricky to meet. This content may just be complex, systems based, or just not presented in the right way. The first technique is to focus on the learning goals of the simulation, especially when the learning goals have been unmet using conventional approaches.

2. Be Part of a Bigger Strategy

Somewhere, right now, a formal or informal team is working on trying to solve your school's biggest perceived challenges. Is it enrollment? Satisfaction of distance deployed programs? Richness and integrity of student body cultures? Find that group, listen to them, and figure out how sims can be a critical piece of the solution.

Many organizations use *Second Life* for fund-raising. This can be directly, by having a large event in world, or indirectly, by showing slides of students using *Second Life* and touting future-oriented activities. There are at least two benefits to this. First, these initiatives have budget. The whole department or school will be rooting for you. They will support you. And more importantly, that will ensure that what you do matters, and that the success of the program matters.

3. Clarify Concepts to Deans

There are plenty of misconceptions floating around about educational simulations. For example, they are dumbing down content for the sake of pandering to ADD, computer-game-addled slackers while upsetting parents and alum. Or high interactivity is trendy but vacuous.

Challenge these assumptions. The more people know about the constructs of the different types of simulations, the more they may realize that a new science is being defined—a new way of representing the world, less like the useful but narrow lenses of Marxism or feminism and more like Isaac Newton's structurally transformational *Philosophiae Naturalis Principia Mathematica*. Using simulations is about enriching content, not flattening it.

4. Stress the Shift

The world is different than it was **mumble** years ago. Here are four differences:

- A new type of student, with a unique and tech-centric background, has entered the system.
- Learning by doing is a better model than learning by knowing. Group projects beat sitting in a lecture audience.
- New skills are necessary for the twenty-first century, such as teamwork and use of technology.
- New tools enable new approaches. We can do things that we simply couldn't do before.

5. Present a Tight Project Plan

Create a project plan. Figure out everything in advance. Think of budgets and time frames. Think of dependencies. Build out spreadsheets. Think of personal and critical skills. Think of deployments. Think of measurement techniques and measurements. If you are considering vendors, put them in your plan as well.

Download a copy of a business plan and follow it. The more specifics you have, the more any conversation will move from "can I?" to "how can I?" and even "when Can I?"

A project plan may have:

- Timelines and dependencies
- Critical stages and success criteria
- Resources needed by stage, including funding and personnel
- Talent Required / Roles and responsibilities
- Integration in existing infrastructure
- Marketing

A business plan may further have:

- Needs unmeet by current approaches and strategic opportunities
- Ongoing and evergreen funding models
- Government and other stakeholders
- Philosophies and assumptions
- Benchmarking approaches
- What peers are doing
- Risk assessments and compensation strategies
- Security and continuity planning
- Balanced scorecard metrics
- What is being replaced

6. Use the Right Terms

Use acceptable terms to describe the program. Only 17 percent of respondents in an eLearning Guild survey, for example, believed that *game* is a productive word to use (Wexler et al. 2008). For many it implies testosterone-charged teenage males wasting their time on an Xbox battling with elves or aliens or street gangs, or else unresponsive employees in a solitaire stupor.

Here are some better words (said with a slight smile, acknowledging both the importance and silliness of the entire conversation), especially for parents, deans, and other administrators:

- Use *simulations* or *sims*, not *games*.
- Use *rules*, not *gameplay*.
- Use *immersive* or *compelling*, not *fun*.
- Use *virtual lab*, not *virtual world*.
- Use *student* or *participant*, not *player*.
- Use *practice*, not *replay*.

Having said all of that, some cultures define themselves as innovative and pioneering. If your culture finds the word *game* acceptable, use it.

Finally, no matter what is said or done by us, the term *game* will be around forever. Any war on the word *games* will have the same success as the war on poverty, the war on drugs, or the war on terrorism. It ain't going away (I have been in many conversations where, once the subject of "a better name for these things" surfaced, all productivity ended until the next meal). Our reality is that computer games are a billion-dollar industry, they are the context that all of our new students now bring with them, and the press loves talking about them.

7. Many Classes Have Gotten Great Results

There will never be an absolutely definitive statement, such as "HIVEs always work better than traditional educational model." To make an obvious point, a well-done traditional program will almost always be better than a badly done sim. However, there are many people doing a lot with sims, and virtually everyone is moving ahead with it. This is true from the survey, the case studies, and surrounding anecdotes. No one is backing away from simulations.

A lot of organizations are getting great results. And clearly, the more similar your organization is to the case study, the more it can be used to convince others.

8. Low Risk/Thin Edge of the Wedge

We are used to thinking of immersive environments as a big deal, a high-risk activity. But one approach is to start with the lowest risk scenario possible. Tap your inner accountant. HIVEs can often do the following:

- Get around the expense and inflexibility of video via tools like Flash.
- Be used for free.
- Be available as pay-as-you-go simulations from outside vendors, rather than a costly and time-consuming custom version.
- Use CD-ROMs to get around bandwidth constraints (About a third of audiences prefer them to the Internet as a way of spread content.)
- Save students time by using a simulation instead of using up class time.
- Leverage existing work in face-to-face classroom simulations.
- Help expand the success of lab simulations into other areas.

Given that a common perception of highly interactive virtual environments is that they are expensive, showing how efficient they are can be a good counterargument.

9. Just Try One

Many HIVEs are short enough, cheap enough, easy enough, and palatable enough not to require permission. Try it out, and once the processes and results are in, show off the results.

10. Do Something Else Well, Earn Credibility, and Then Spend It

Credibility is your most important currency. Build it by successfully completing almost any earlier program. Show the results.

But it is not enough just to have credibility. You have to actively invest it. You have to say, "I will make this work," or "This is going to have a great impact on the students." Department heads and deans know that success happens when people put their reputation on the line. By the way, this is hard. Many people are much better at earning credibility than spending it.

WHAT DOES SUCCESS LOOK LIKE FOR YOU?

There are a lot of approaches here, and you may easily have quite a few better ones. It comes down to this: Imagine you are standing in front of a roomful of colleagues and educational leaders. You show a single slide that shows two lines on chart—a before and an after line. The before line is trending downward, while the after line is trending upward.

In your perfect world, what are the labels of those charts? Is it test scores, attendance, student satisfaction scores, or external press references? Whatever it is that you and your organization most value, use that as the impetus and drive towards it. It is different for everybody.

Epilogue: The New Attraction of Distance Learning

It wasn't that long ago that distance deployed in classrooms felt second-class to face-to-face. It was viewed with suspicion and distrust by a hiring HR department. College administrations in ivy-covered halls must have had a good laugh at the early quality of instruction and interaction. And it probably seemed as self-evident to many that the co-located students and classes would necessarily have richer interactions and higher-quality experiences than those far-flung all over the globe. What is interesting, however, is this might be changing. We may be arriving at a time when far-flung classrooms actually have long-term inherent infrastructural *advantages* over co-located ones.

There is of course the cost. Not having to worry about "room and board" makes so many schools so much more attractive. But another big advantage is the opportunity for diversity of students (which also comes in part from lower cost). People who are twenty years old can be a student with someone who is eighty years old. Further, and incredibly, people's experiences and even contexts are so much more diverse. In the same classroom on organizational behavior, one person could have just been in a firefight in Afghanistan and another in a boardroom meeting in Detroit (in his or her own firefight).

Just one not so surprising datum point is that the number of distributed learning programs using simulations is increasing. Fully one-third of professors learning about Capsim business simulations are now planning to use them in a distributed classroom, according to Dan Smith, founder and president of Capsim. Simulations add interactivity. They drive emotional engagement and provide a shared context for chat rooms.

But there may be an even more surprising conclusion. *It may be easier to use simulations in a virtual classroom environment than one that is face to face.*

I'd thought the opposite. I had thought face-to-face would be much easier for one big reason: students who were confused would have access to immediate help. It turns out that I both underestimated students and overestimated the face-to-face learning environment.

The thing that is holding up so many deployments in a classroom college environment is the less-than-100-percent access to computers. There are plenty of desks and plenty of chairs and inspirational posters but an uneven distribution of laptops and desktops. Even if everyone has a laptop, getting them all in the same room is tough.

In contrast, in a virtual environment, an instructor can be completely assured that every single student has a computer on in front of them. And yes, students are more than capable of solving their own technical issues. The riff has been that virtual classes are inferior to face-to-face for so long that many of us haven't noticed a subtle shift. Now, hopefully the land-locked schools will rise to the occasion and get competitive.

REFERENCES

Aldrich, C. 2009. *The complete guide to simulations and serious games.* San Francisco: Jossey-Bass/Pfeiffer.

Aldrich, C. 2005. *Learning by doing.* San Francisco: Jossey-Bass/Pfeiffer.

Barrie, E. 2001. Meaningful interpretive experiences from the participants' perspective. PhD diss., Indiana University.

Bloomfield, R. 2007. *Metanomics.* http://www.metanomics.net

Crawford, C. 1984. *The art of computer game design.* Berkeley, CA: Osborne/McGraw-Hill.

Csikszentmihalyi, M. 1990. *Flow: The psychology of optimum experience.* New York: Harper Perennial.

Gee, J. P. 2003. *What video games have to teach us about learning and literacy.* New York: Palgrave/Macmillan.

Habgood, M.P.J., S. E. Ainsworth, and S. Benford. 2005. Endogenous fantasy and learning in digital games. *Simulation and Gaming 36* (4): 483–498.

Held, R., and A. Hein. 1963. Movement-produced stimulation in the development of visually guided behavior. *Journal of Comparative and Physiological Psychology 56,* 872–876.

Kapp, K. 2007. *Gadgets, games, and gizmos for learning: Tools and techniques for transforming know-how from boomers to gamers.* San Francisco: Jossey-Bass/Pfeiffer.

Keith, N., and M. Frese. 2008. Effectiveness of error management training: A meta-analysis. *Journal of Applied Psychology 93,* 59–69.

Kiili, K. 2005. Digital game-based learning: Towards an experiential gaming model. *The Internet and Higher Education 8* (1): 13–24.

Kirriemuir, J. 2005. March. Presentation at Serious Games Summit, Game Developers Conference, San Francisco.

Klein, T. A., T. Endrass, N. Kathmann, J. Neumann, D. Y. von Cramon, and M. Ullsperger. 2007. Neural correlates of error awareness. *NeuroImage 34* (4), 1774–1781.

Ledoux, J. 1998. *The emotional brain.* New York: Simon & Schuster.

Lepper, M. R., and T. W. Malone. 1987. Intrinsic motivation and instructional effectiveness in computer-based education. In *Conative and affective process analysis,* ed. R. E. Snow and M. J. Farr, 223–243. Hillsdale, NJ: Erlbaum.

Senge, P. M. 1990. *The fifth discipline: The art and practice of the learning organization.* New York: Currency Doubleday.

Squire, K., M. Barnett, J. M. Grant, and T. Higginbotham. 2004. *Electromagnetism supercharged! Learning physics with digital simulation games.* (Proceedings of the 2004 International Conference of the Learning Sciences). Los Angeles: UCLA Press.

Wexler, S., K. Corti, A. Derryberry, C. Quinn, and A. van Barneveld. 2008. *360 report: Immersive learning situations 2008: The demand for, and demands of, simulations, scenarios, and serious games.* Santa Rosa, CA: eLearning Guild.

Yukl, G. 2002. *Power and influence in leadership in organizations.* 5th ed. Chapter 6. Upper Saddle River, NJ: Prentice Hall,

INDEX

Page references followed by *fig* indicate an illustrated figure; followed by *t* indicate a table.

A

HIVEs adoption strategies (*continued*)
project plan, 117–118; 6. use the right terms,
118–119; 7. citing many classes have gotten
great results, 119; 8. low risk/thin edge of
the wedge, 119; 9. just try one, 120; 10. do
something else well, earn credibility, and
then spent it, 120

HIVEs components: context and emotional
involvement as, 6; games as a learning tool,
5; participation as, 6

HIVEs culture: etiquette rules of, 39–40;
frustration-anticipate resolution pairing of,
40–42; instructor's learning to not interfere
characteristic of, 42–43; interactivity
of, 15–20; making emotional states
explicit characteristic of, 40; synchronous
conversations experience of, 39–40

HIVEs (Highly Interactively Virtual
Environments): building credibility of,
120; clarifying what is meant by, 6–14;
components of, 5–6; correct terminology
used to describe, 118; costs associated with
using, 53–54, 61*t*, 62, 117–118; culture
of interactivity of, 15–20; curriculum
incorporation of already available, 53;
examining the learning value of, 4;
explaining why learning is facilitated by, 5;
growing interest in and future applications
of, 121–122; illustrated diagram of, 8*fig*;
making curriculum decisions on, 48–53;
off-the-shelf, 59–63; role of coaching in,
89–102; technology accessible by students
issue, 63–65. *See also* Virtual environments

I

IBM, 48
Ice-breaker activity, 13
Infrastructure selection criteria: instructor
controls, 65; *Second Life* classrooms, 65–66;
technology accessible by most students, 63–65
Instant messaging, 56
Institutions: building support for HIVE use
by, 116–120; HIVEs and associated costs for,
53–54*t*, 61*t*, 62; interactive curriculum used
by, 49–54*t*; interactive environments used by,
3–4; internal development group of, 61

Instructional Design and Technology
(University of North Dakota), 59
Instruction decisions: content selection criteria
for, 66–69; on how to access content, 55–63;
infrastructure selection criteria for, 63–66;
on self-paced/single player, asynchronous,
or synchronous, 69–71; trust as factor in, 71
Instructor prep work: accessing the
content, 55–63; chunking content,
76–80*fig*; connecting with other interested
professionals, 55; content selection criteria,
66–69; infrastructure selection criteria, 63–66;
piloting, 81–83; self-paced/single player,
asynchronous, or synchronous decisions,
69–71; technical support for students, 67,
75–76; trust as selection criterion, 71
Instructors: building support for HIVEs,
116–120; creating evaluation strategies,
103–112; learning to not interfere, 42–43;
list of concerns about adopting simulations
by, 115–116; necessary preparation required
of, 43; support materials by, 66–68, 78–80*fig*;
technical support provided by, 67, 75–76;
virtual environment ability to control
or gate, 65. *See also* After action reviews
(AARs); *Second Life* coaching; Students
Interactive curriculum: accessing real-world
communities, 50; using already available
HIVEs for, 53; building credibility of,
120; building support for HIVEs and,
116–120; costs associated with HIVEs,
53–54*t*, 61*fig*–62, 117–118; creating sense
of presence through virtual worlds, 49–50;
using educational simulations for critical
content, 53; using games, 50–51; increasing
knowledge using, 51–53; providing access to
labs and props, 51, 52*fig. See also* Content;
Pedagogical elements
Interactive spreadsheets: description of, 32–34;
originally created by professors, 62; screen
shot of, 33*fig*
Interactivity: enabling, 15–16; game levels
of, 17–19; leadership models and levels of,
19–20; learning goals of true, 15;
pre-game levels of, 16–17; when to include
curriculum, 49–53

P

Participants. *See* Students

Pedagogical elements: definition of, 25; overlap of simulation, game, and, 27*fig*; simulation elements mixed with, 23; A Virtual Coach Gives Players Advice example of, 26. *See also* Content; Didactic elements; Interactive curriculum

Peer assessment, 108–109

Philosophiae Naturalis Principia Mathematica (Newton), 117

Piloting: communication infrastructure, 82–83; conceptual, 83; description and function of, 81; technical, 81

PlayStations, 65

Poser, 57

Practiceware, 34

Prep work. *See* Instructor prep work

Printed workbooks/guides, 78–80*fig*

professor-created simulations, 62

Props access, 51, 52*fig*

ProtonMedia, 15, 56, 57

Protosphere, 8, 15, 48, 56

R

Reading recommendations, 67

Results: building HIVEs support by pointing out, 119; example of, 23; simulation element representing, 22

Robo Rush, 35*fig*–36*fig*

Role-plays, 70

Roller Coaster Tycoon, 63

RSS feeds, 57

S

Saulnier, D., 68, 82, 101

Schools. *See* Institutions

Second Life: behavior changes evidenced in, 50; classroom choices in, 65–66; cost options of university use of, 54; games used within, 13; instructor exploration of and presence in, 55; interfacing other sims to, 71–73; learning facilitated through, 72–73; multiplayer format of, 70, 71, 86, 95–97; popularity of, 56–57; recommendations for approaches institutional use of, 57; student modification of

environment, 110; synchronous conversations culture of, 39–40; unstructured virtual world of, 7, 8; as virtual world standard, 55–57. *See also* Virtual worlds

Second Life coaching: after action reviews (AARs) as part of, 99–101; benefits of highlighting mistakes of one group, 98; on competitors and competition, 96–97; first public simulation play, 93–94; grouping approaches taken by, 95–96; the intellectual setup, 91; managing the bottom 20players, 99; multiplayer or team-based sims, 70, 71, 86, 95–97; "off ramp" taking students back to real life, 101–102; ongoing player comparison while, 98–99; ongoing tracking and questioning roles of, 97–98; "on ramp" taking students from real life to simulation, 92–93; perfect play, good enough, or intentional failure goal of, 94–95; providing extra bonus challenges for top 20players, 98; remember to not adjust the settings, 90; right amount of hand-holding while, 97; setting the tone, 91–92; the setup, 89–90; softly bringing people into *Second Life,* 90; teaching the interface, 93. *See also* Instructors; Student engagement; Students

Self-paced/single player game. *See* Single player games

Serious games: educational simulation versus, 10–12; examples of, 11*t*; illustrated diagram of, 7, 8*fig*; *SimCity* as, 10–11, 12

SharePoint, 57

Shea, P., 85–88

SimCity, 10–11, 12, 59, 63

Sim examples: branching story, 32*fig*; Chatting in a Virtual World, 49*fig*; An Interactive Spreadsheet from Virtual University, 33*fig*; key concept review in My Sim, 30*fig*; playing the sims while other sims are playing a game, 72*fig*; *Robo Rush* minigame, 35*fig*–36*fig*; throttle in bottom of boat sim, 22*fig*; A Virtual Coach Gives Players Advice, 26*fig*

The Sims, 7, 68, 69

Sims: accessing stand-alone, 58; Adobe Flash-based, 48, 52*fig*, 59, 64; availability of free, 59; chunking content through, 76–78; description of, 21; game elements used

TITLES IN THE JOSSEY-BASS ONLINE TEACHING AND LEARNING SERIES

Conquering the Content: A Step-by-Step Guide to Online Course Design
By: Robin M. Smith
ISBN: 978-0-7879-9442-6

Assessing the Online Learner: Resources and Strategies for Faculty
By: Rena M. Palloff and Keith Pratt
ISBN: 978-0-470-28386-8

Collaborating Online: Learning Together in Community
By: Rena M. Palloff and Keith Pratt
ISBN: 978-0-7879-7614-9

Using Wikis for Online Collaboration: The Power of the Read-Write Web
By: James A. West and Margaret L. West
ISBN: 978-0-470-34333-3

Engaging the Online Learner: Activities and Resources for Creative Instruction
By: Rita-Marie Cohen and J. Ana Davidson
ISBN: 978-0-7879-6667-6

Learning in Real Time: Synchronous Teaching and Learning Online
By: Jonathan E. Finkelstein
ISBN: 978-0-7879-7921-8

Exploring the Digital Library: A Guide for Online Teaching and Learning
By: Kay Johnson and Elaine Maqusin
ISBN: 978-0-7879-7627-9

The Online Teaching and Learning Tool Kit - *a 20% package discount*
ISBN: 978-0-470-38053-6
Includes: *Learning in Real Time, Collaborating Online, Engaging the Online Learner, Assessing the Online Learner, and Conquering the Content*

Attend our online conference based around the series,
The Jossey-Bass Online Teaching and Learning Conference - Online
www.OnlineTeachingandLearning.com